FIRESIDE

FRIDAY NIGHT POKER

Drawings by *CARL ROSÉ*

or Penny Poker for Millions

by IRV RODDY

A Fireside Book Published by
Simon and Schuster · New York

ISBN 0–671–21348–2
LIBRARY OF CONGRESS CATALOG CARD NUMBER 61–14028
MANUFACTURED IN THE UNITED STATES OF AMERICA

8 9 10 11 12 13 14 15 16 17

FOR
Barbara
Gerald
Amy

Contents

Acknowledgments

There comes the time after the galleys of a book are corrected when you can hardly believe that it is over. You sit back and wait and think of the people who helped in so many different ways.

There are the hundreds I have met at the table for more years than need be noted. Those I play with now will remember the occasions when I scribbled a hand on the back of an envelope, for most of the exhibits and problems are actual hands. I thank them all. Who is Freddie? He is all of us—at times!

How I must have bored my non-poker-playing friends with all sorts of tales. To them I add my apologies.

Pat Powell typed the final draft. She demonstrated the patience of a poker pro. Dorothy Richardson assisted in the typing.

At occasional points in the text I referred to my mathematician friends—Joe Waksberg and George Heller. George checked the logic and computations of all the problems and edited the entire manuscript. He must have walked off with the spelling prizes, too.

There is always the spouse who inspired it all. Gussie goaded me into starting. Then she typed the first draft, edited it, and made many important contributions throughout the project.

And now on to poker, for "the game's the thing."

—I.R.

1

So You're
a Poker Player

Is it fun playing poker? It sure is. It's even more fun to play poker and win. If you don't agree, this book is not for you. It was written for your buddy Al, who enjoys winning. He read every page twice, but he didn't need to read the book at all. He outplays you, outsmarts you and outmaneuvers you every Friday night. He talks you into some pots and out of others. Even more important, he listens better than you do. He rarely bluffs, but you think he does. Last Friday you asked if the seven spot Herb folded was a heart. No one answered; Al knew it was a heart. The cigarette between his lips twitched. You learned nothing. He learned a lot about your hand.

You play poker for small stakes every Friday night, with an occasional miss, but you squeeze in a few extras during the year with another group. You average four hours each session. It comes to about 200 hours of poker each year. You can read this book in about two and one half or three hours. Might as well;

what can you lose? Read it on Thursday. No need to miss a session. But don't mention it to the boys; it's enough that Al knows.

There aren't many books on poker. The few there are deal largely with table stakes, no limit or pot limit. The games covered are draw poker and five-card stud. There is a section, usually a short one, on seven-card stud. Seven-card high-low is worth only a couple of pages. Well, what about small-stakes-limit poker? If you find anything, it will be only a few paragraphs here and there.

This is a form of poker snobbery in poker books that doesn't make any sense. The vast majority of poker played in the U.S. is seven-card stud, high-low games, and wild-card games with low-limit stakes. They are Friday- or Saturday-nighters, every week or two. The stakes are 5 and 10 cents; 10, 15 and 25; 10, 25 and 50; 25 and 50 cents; or some similar combination in the less-than-a-dollar range. Indeed, penny games are perhaps the most frequent for a sociable weekend evening in the suburbs.

Here is what this book is about. It describes and analyzes a few games in considerable detail. They are the best games I know. "Best" means those requiring the most ability; they are also the most entertaining. Most poker books are superficial about the middle rounds and end game. Not this book. A number of other high-low and wild-card games are also reviewed in less detail. The study of many deceptive tactics is a major feature. Most important, the book is mainly concerned with low-stakes (less than $1) limit poker. Millions of people play in this range. Very few play at the higher prices. Finally, this book contains many illustrative hands; there are probably more poker hands and poker problems here than in all other poker books combined.

Table stakes (or no-limit poker) is a serious, gambling, cutthroat business, usually involving large sums. My experiences at this type of poker have been trying. It's harder than working. It is played by grim, salty characters; let the novice beware! The difference between table stakes and limit poker is mainly the consequence of the narrow, predetermined range in the amount that can be bet in a limit game, and the unlimited range that can be bet at table stakes or no-limit poker.

A 5, 10 and 15 cents dealer's-choice game is an amiable mixture of gambling, skill, kibitzing and sociability for most players. There is certainly an occasional sweat because it is money and you want to win. Luck may override ability in one or even a few sessions. In the long run the skill shows.

If you are not familiar with table-stakes five-card stud, you have a lot of company, for it is rarely played. Who can afford it? Let's review it briefly. In some respects five-card-stud table stakes is a simpler game than high-low seven-card stud at 25 cents, 50 cents and a dollar. I think it can be demonstrated that it's simpler insofar as card skill is concerned. The bluff, rather than card skill, is the key in table stakes. Consider this point. Which of the two games mentioned has more card variables? No question about this: seven-card high-low. You can record in a few lines what you should stay on for the first bet in five-card-stud table stakes. It's not so in seven-card high-low. Why? More variables to consider; therefore more card skill. And some of the games described later have even more variables than seven-card high-low.

In table stakes you may bet any amount you have on the table. You are not permitted to add to that amount or reduce that amount during the play of a hand. Money is the main instrument of play rather than cards. One important feature can be observed. The player with the larger bankroll has a great advantage over a player with a substantially lesser amount. Suppose you sit in a six-man game and have brought along the seventy bucks you stashed away for this occasion. Your spouse thinks you are out for an evening of penny poker with the boys, but you're really playing 10, 25 and 50 cents poker. Each of the other five players has brought $1,000 and places it on the table. Are you concerned? Not at all. Seventy is ample for this game. A swing of $50 or $60 is big. Now consider table stakes with the same sums involved. You might as well drop 69 on the table and dash off to the local movie house. The show may give you a laugh. The poker game will give you a headache, and your $70 will be gone before you start.

As most table-stakes hands are two-man games after the first or second up card, let's consider a two-player hand. You are playing with a stranger. The cards are dealt.

	Down	Up
You	K	Q
Opponent	?	9

You bet $1. Opponent calls.

	Down	Up	
You	K	Q	K
Opponent	?	9	J

You bet $5. Opponent calls.

	Down	Up		
You	K	Q	K	6
Opponent	?	9	J	A

Opponent checks. You bet $5. He calls.

	Down	Up				
You	K	Q	K	6	2	
Opponent	?	9	J	A	4	Last card

At this point you have $59 remaining. Opponent has $989. There is $22 in the pot, as there was no ante. Opponent bets $59!

It is now your turn to call or fold. If you call and lose you are finished, and you can't even afford that movie.

Let's go back and study the hand again. On the first bet of $1, opponent called quickly. At the second bet he called slowly. Did he react in this way because you took your time? You were deciding how large a bet he would stand without folding after you drew that lovely Kowboy. You say you don't play slowly. Don't be an ass. Of course you do. Table-stakes poker is always played slowly. Do you remember the previous hand when you dropped out after a long huddle with a 6 in the hole and a 9 up? What were you thinking of then? No, the redhead at the switchboard is thirty-eight at least.

So why did he call slowly? Was he thinking of folding? Was he thinking of raising? Maybe he has seen "red" and has the same problem.

At the next bet he looked at the ceiling for a while, then checked. He called your $5 bet. Did he buy aces? Is this consistent with his early play? Maybe there was a fly on the ceiling. His slow action here could have been an act, which is perfectly proper in poker. He may have been considering betting or deciding whether to trap with aces.

After the last card your problem is in spades. Only an ace as Mr. O's closed card can beat you. If you lose you are finished for the night! So you groan awhile and finally decide. Does it matter? Not much. You'll have to win a few of these without losing a single one before you can hope to survive this night.

If you had a thousand in front of you it wouldn't be so bad. You could either call or fold. If you call and lose, there are more to come and you may get a "lock" on him the next pot. If I had started with $70 and knew nothing about O's style or ability, I would have the same headache you are having. With the thousand I would call. Here is why. He can only have an ace or a 9 in the hole. In table stakes you stay for the first bet only when you beat all hands in sight. If he had an ace in the hole he would probably fold at the first $5 bet. He would have only one card higher than your K Q in sight. The pot has only $2. He would probably fold the A J 9. In fact he was thinking of folding the 9s on the grounds that the pot was so small compared to the bet. After the last card, he realized it was a good bluffing situation because you were so obviously scared of going home early. If you had a big bundle he may not have bet so strongly.

So you see, the amounts of money bet are as important, or more important, than the cards in table stakes. Knowledge of probabilities, recall of all folded cards, ability to interpret mannerisms and comments, knowledge of habits of particular players and deceptive tactics of various types sum up to a poker player's card ability, but there is still a huge element of

random action by your opponent brought about by the vast
range in the size of bet he can make. In this game a good player
must bluff in a somewhat random pattern. Bluffing in other
ways might be detected by a shrewd player. When your opponent does make a really large bet—let us say three times the
amount already in the pot—your card skill usually becomes a
small feature compared with the random element, unless he is
an absolute fool and you know it and can use the information.
He may be a fool and you may not know it; or he may be a fool
and you may not be able to use the information. This is particularly critical when you play table stakes with a relatively
small sum.

Consider this somewhat analogous circumstance. You are
living in a country where there is no income tax on money won
gambling, nor does a gambling loss result in a tax refund. You
have one million dollars. You have just retired to a life of luxury
and leisure. (When you've got it, it's pronounced "lĕs/zure.")
Along comes a nut. This is a special kind of nut with $20,000,000
who likes to toss coins for large sums. He offers to lay 2 to 1 on the
toss of a truly honest coin. Will he lay you $2,000 to $1,000 on
repetitive tosses? This would be the equivalent of his giving
you $500 on every toss. You could make about $2,000,000 a
day—with an honest coin. About twelve hours of fast tossing
would just about do it.

But he is not that kind of nut. He offers to bet you $2,000,000
to $1,000,000 on one toss, all honest and duly supervised. Well,
this nut may be the same person that bet $59 on that hand of
poker with a pair of 9s or he may not. This time we know
the guy is a fool, but I would be unable to take advantage
of this fool.

Why? I am not going to risk my million. That incremental
$2,000,000 has a small value to me, compared with the prospect
of being broke. Ownership of $3,000,000 is a lot better than
$1,000,000, I imagine, but the contrast between $0 and $1,000,000
is far greater.

I might risk a half million on the 2-to-1 chance. Maybe even $900,000 after assuring myself that it is an honest toss, but not that last $100,000. I might even risk it, but not for a mere 2-to-1 advantage. In short, each additional dollar a person owns has a different marginal value than every other dollar.

You see now that you may be playing with a fool, but if he has ten or twenty times as much money as you, his being a fool may not help you at table stakes. You get him in a $2-limit, dealer's-choice game and you'll shred him like cabbage.

A few personal comments. I started the poker bit almost thirty years ago at my mother's elbow, whenever I was permitted to watch. From her I first learned the mysteries and fascinations of poker and the dignity of people and card games requiring skill and imagination. Later as a teen-ager I played wherever I could—in cellar clubs, in hallways, the sandpile at Lawson Playground, Chicago. In the Army days, I played for high stakes. An Australian pound was $3.20 in U. S. money, but we treated it like a dollar. Japanese yen had the stature of paper. In November 1945 we were quartered in a huge warehouse called the Silk Mill. A five-card-stud, pot-limit poker game was in progress. As the going price for a carton of cigarettes in Tokyo and Yokohama was 200 yen, everyone in the game was loaded. The first bet was normally 50 yen. The final bet in the average pot was usually between 500 and 1,000 yen. The funny little papers were changing hands rapidly. The rate of exchange was 15 yen to $1 U. S. The opening bet was almost $3 and the final bet was usually in the $40-to-$70 range. Most of the guys in the outfit had been overseas for two years. We had been relieved of duty and were leaving for the States in a few days. The men in the outfit were called to exchange our Japanese money for U. S. currency in preparation for our departure. The poker game was interrupted for maybe an hour. We reassembled and the cards were dealt. A young fellow from Springfield, Massachusetts, was high. He reached into his pocket: "Bet a half dollar." A little while ago he had been betting wildly—$5, $10, $50—but in yen. Now it was the real green stuff and he and all the rest of us settled down to conservative betting.

I played a little tournament bridge from 1946 to 1949. I couldn't find a poker game. Since 1949 I have played poker regularly. I never played high-low games until that year, but I immediately enjoyed them better than the standard brands of poker. I realized that the high-low games required more skill.

So remember, poker is a great game. It is even greater when you win.

2

Down
the River

Seven-card stud, also known as "down the river," is a game with enough zip to satisfy exotic tastes. It requires card-reading ability, recall of cards that have been folded, attention to the probabilities. It is full of uncertainty and has a vast range for deception.

Each player receives three cards before the first bet is made. Two are dealt closed and one open. After the first round of betting another open card is dealt and so on until players who have remained in the pot have two closed cards and four open cards. The seventh card is dealt down and the hand is completed with another bet.

Consider first the problem of staying on the first bet. Suppose you are dealt K♠ and 9♡ down and 8♣ up. The player to your right is high and bets 10 cents. What should you do? If you answer "call" or if you answer "fold" you are wrong! You have failed to consider the fact that the evaluation of your hand at

25

each point is relative and the amount already in the pot at any particular point must influence your action. You did not have all the pertinent information. The correct response to the question "What should you do?" should have been "How much did we ante?" If there was no ante of any kind, you should clearly get out. If each of six players plunked down a fat dollar for the first three cards, you should call for 10 cents with K♠, 9♡ and 8♣.

Another aspect of the problem that warrants attention is the attitude or style of the players in the game. If all of the others play a tight, cautious brand of poker, you'll be badly beaten if you play loosely. On the other hand, if you play overly tight while the others play a loose, friendly sort of game you'll probably win, but it will also be the last time you are invited to that game. You cannot expect another invitation to a loose game when you play it cozy. Most of the games you are in will be loosely played, so there is no need to play too close. In a high-stakes game, of course, you must play carefully. Suppose the stakes permit bets of $1 to $5. If they don't invite you back, that is tough. You must play each hand with grave regard for the cost, the chances of improving your hand, and the reward for holding the highest hand. Most of the others will be playing tight in a high-stakes game anyway.

I'll give some general standards and considerations on the first action shortly. You should, however, vary these to fit the situation. If it is a comfortable neighborhood game where everyone stays on almost any excuse, you can stay on even worse hands than the optional situations described later. If it is a high-stakes game or a cautious game, you must play accordingly.

The problem of the first action is discussed in some detail in most books on poker, but the standards set down are rigid and too severe, in my view. One writer on the subject * states

* Herbert O. Yardley, *The Education of a Poker Player*, Simon and Schuster, New York, 1957, p. 84.

that his requirements for calling the first bet in seven-card stud will result in playing in one pot out of seven. Assume that everyone in the game has read the same book and been impressed by the author's persuasiveness or promise of riches and is using the same standards. A little more arithmetic for which my mathematician friends have a fancy name, binomial expansions, gives us these facts. The expected results for the following events in a six-handed game, if each player's prospects are considered independently, are:

(1) 39.7% of the time none of the players in the game will have the requirements for staying in! This is two out of five deals! Did you ask what happens to the ante in center of table? I have been wondering too!

(2) Another 39.7% of the time one player has the requirements. He must get the ante! There is no contest in eight of ten deals.

(3) In 16.5% of the pots (one in six), two players stay for the first bet. In some situations, you are instructed to drop on the next card unless you improve.

(4) 3.7% of the time (four pots in a hundred) you'll have three players after the first bet.

(5) In about 0.5%, or one deal in 200, you'll have four or more players after the first round.

This is poker? Of course not. It's a game called "Who Gets the Ante" or "Shuffling and Dealing Is Fun." A wise guy in this game could steal the ante hand after hand.

Another book on poker* gives even tighter standards for the first-card action, but discusses, in other parts of the book, endgame situations in which four players remain. It would hardly ever happen.

Are you confused? The answer to this riddle is that practically

---

* Irwin Steig, *Poker for Fun and Profit*, McDowell Obolensky, Inc., New York, 1959, pp. 111, 112.

no one plays so tight that he stays to the first bet only one time in seven. Should you find a stranger in your midst who plays this way, there are several things you can do to protect yourself. First make a mental note to be sure this character isn't invited next time. Then needle him about continuously folding. When he finally stays in a pot, be sure to drop out *very* conspicuously with a suitable comment—"Can't buck three of a kind with my small pair." The idea will spread rapidly to the others in your game and he will leave shortly. Don't worry about his feelings. Worry instead about the contents of your wallet and the amiability of your game. Besides, this character has thick skin. He'll survive. If he doesn't leave early, you can suggest a drastic increase in the size of the ante.

Here are some standards for the first bet in seven-card stud. Remember you must use judgment in the optional calls and make other adjustments to fit your game. Call the first round on any of the following:

a. Three of a kind
b. Three in sequence
c. Three in a suit
d. Pair of aces, kings or queens with any additional card
e. Any other pair with an ace or king as the kicker
f. Any pair with queen or lower card as the kicker
g. A, K, X or A, Q, X with two in the same suit
   (small card may be anything)

The hands described above are sound first-round calls. You can also stand a raise on a. through e. On f. and g. you should call, but if there is a raise before it becomes your turn, your action must be reconsidered. You should fold if any weakening factor exists, if there was no ante or if it is a tough game. A weakening factor is the exposure in another hand of the card you have paired, or of any other critical card in your hand.

Some optional first-round calls are:

h.	A, K, X	assorted suits, X represents any low card
i.	A, Q, X	assorted suits
j.	A, X, X	when two are of same suit and ace is not exposed in another hand
k.	K, J, X	when two are of same suit and king is not exposed elsewhere
l.	K, Q, 10	any suits
m.	A, 6, 7	any suits with two small cards in sequence and ace not exposed
n.	Q, 10, 9	with no jacks in sight (but not 9, 7, 6)

A few other similar types of holdings may be treated as optional in a loose game, particularly if luck seems to be running your way. If you are losing, you must tighten up. Luck will average out in the long run. Be patient.

Some important factors may be noted in connection with the standards described. A hand containing three deuces or better will frequently win. Two pair with aces over is also a rather good holding and will win a good share of pots. Kings over is on the strong side. Queens over is getting into the losing range, especially when there has been some raising. The target in determining your first action is a hand with a good or tolerable chance of making kings over or better. Where queen is the high card, there must be some other good developmental possibility (see n.). Thus A, 8, 4 is a better start than Q, 10, 8, if both are assorted suits. Two small pair is a trap holding in this game. You stay to the end at considerable expense. It doesn't win very often and has a small chance of improving.

On all of the optional situations, if a raise is made before you have called, you should fold unless the ante is high. In that case, some of the stronger hands in the optional list may be worth staying for one more card. On borderline hands an important feature is that your key cards be down. Thus A♡, K♡

down and 3♠ up is better than K♡, 3♠ down and A♡ up. If the
hand improves, you'll be in a position to win a larger pot with
your strength hidden.

Your action after the fourth card depends upon the card you
receive, your opponents' exposed cards, the size of the bet, the
size of the pot, potential raises in back of you, and an intangible
factor that may be called "command of the table." We'll play a
couple of hands to study fourth-card and end-game situations.

Conditions: 10-cent ante; 10, 20 and 30-cent limit; 10 cents
              first bet, 20 cents second and third bets, and 30
              cents on last two bets or open pair on second or
              third bet. We'll play a quiet, family game and
              outlaw check and raise and other forms of sand-
              bagging.

	Down		Up
A	10♡	Q♠	10♣
B	7♠	7◊	9♠
C	4♣	Q♡	5♠
D	9♡	9◊	J♡
E	A♡	K♡	J♠
F	8♣	7♡	10◊
G	J♣	10♠	5♣

G is the dealer in these hands
D is high and bets 10 cents
E calls
F calls
G folds
A calls
B calls
C folds

Comment: In my book, F should have folded, especially with
           the exposed 9. You'll find the majority of players in
           on this hand, but it is distinctly a losing play.

4th card

	Down		Up		
A	10♡	Q♠	10♣	3♡	No improvement
B	7♠	7♢	9♠	3♠	Three spades
D	9♡	9♢	J♡	3♢	No improvement
E	A♡	K♡	J♠	4♡	Three hearts
F	8♣	7♡	10♢	5♡	A weirdy. Now needing a 6 or 9

E is high and bets 20 cents
All others call

F is still in there chasing.

5th card

	Down		Up			
A	10♡	Q♠	10♣	3♡	6♣	No improvement
B	7♠	7♢	9♠	3♠	6♡	No improvement
D	9♡	9♢	J♡	3♢	J♢	Two pair
E	A♡	K♡	J♠	4♡	K♠	Ace and kings are still very live
F	8♣	7♡	10♢	5♡	2♣	Going nowhere

D is high and bets 30 cents
E calls
F folds
A calls
B calls

D is not excited with his prospects as a J and a 9 are exposed
   in other hands
A should fold
B should fold

6th card

	Down		Up				
A	10♡	Q♠	10♣	3♡	6♣	2♡	Still 10s
B	7♠	7◇	9♠	3♠	6♡	A♠	A four flush
D	9♡	9◇	J♡	3◇	J◇	Q♣	No improvement
E	A♡	K♡	J♠	4♡	K♠	A◇	It is all hidden

D is high and bets 30 cents
E raises to 60 cents
A folds
B calls
D calls

　　　D didn't know what else to do
　　　A gives up, at last

7th card

	Down		Up				Down	
B	7♠	7◇	9♠	3♠	6♡	A♠	8♡	No help
D	9♡	9◇	J♡	3◇	J◇	Q♣	K◇	No help
E	A♡	K♡	J♠	4♡	K♠	A◇	2◇	No help

D is high and checks
E bets 30 cents
B folds
D calls

　　　E wins the pot with aces over kings

Here is another hand for examination:

	Down		Up
A	6♠	9♡	3♡
B	2♢	Q♡	2♣
C	5♠	A♢	K♢
D	4♠	Q♢	10♢
E	10♣	7♣	3♠
F	J♢	A♣	J♣
G	9♣	J♡	7♢

C is high and bets 10 cents

D calls

E folds

F calls

G folds

A folds

B calls

D should have folded with no ace or king

G's action is correct. This is no play for a straight.

4th card

	Down		Up		
B	2♢	Q♡	2♣	7♠	No help
C	5♠	A♢	K♢	8♢	Three diamonds
D	4♠	Q♢	10♢	7♡	No help
F	J♢	A♣	J♣	6♡	No help

C is high and bets 20 cents

D folds

F calls

B calls

B might have folded, but in last position I will not quarrel

5th card

	Down		Up			
B	2♦	Q♡	2♣	7♠	10♡	No help
C	5♠	A♦	K♦	8♦	5♣	Small pair
F	J♦	A♣	J♣	6♡	Q♠	No help

C is still high and bets 20 cents
F calls
B folds

B must fold at this point. A call to the fifth card is critical
in seven-card stud, as it nearly always results in a call on the
next card. If the hand finally improves to two small pair, it
is even more expensive.

6th card

C	draws 8♣	Two pair
F	draws 9♦	No help

C bets 30 cents
F calls

7th card

C	draws A♠	He holds aces over
F	draws J♠	He holds three jacks

C is high and bets 30 cents
F raises to 60 cents
C calls

Three jacks wins

These were typical run-of-the-mill hands. A flush bucking a
full house doesn't occur very often.

There are ten hands listed below. Look them over and decide
what you would do with each of them. Conditions are the same as
earlier in this chapter. Some modifications will be noted as we
proceed.

The player to your right is high with a king of spades and bets a dime. The exposed cards of other players are 2♡, Q♣, J◇, 5♡, and 4◇. You have put a dime in for the ante.

	Down		Up		Down		Up
1.	K♡	9♠	8♡	6.	A♡	8◇	K♣
2.	8♠	Q♠	3♣	7.	6♣	A◇	3♡
3.	2◇	K◇	8♣	8.	9◇	9♣	6♠
4.	10♡	A♠	10◇	9.	A♠	A♣	J♣
5.	6♡	9♡	10♣	10.	K♣	J♣	6♣

1. K is weakened but you have two in sequence and two to a flush. I would drop but would not quarrel with a call if you feel in a sporting mood. However, if you do call you must improve on the next card. Remember that the next round is 20 cents and there is always the possibility of a raise in back of you.

2. You must fold. The chances of developing a winner are very poor. Remember the objective is a holding with a good chance of developing a hand consisting of kings over or better. You will sometimes win with a poorer hand and may lose with a better hand. Nevertheless, this is a good working objective.

3. Not good enough. You must fold. A king is exposed.

4. This is a good start. No 10s or aces are exposed. Always, and I mean always, consider the exposed cards in determining your action.

5. Fold. Don't let the possibility of a straight or flush suck you in. You *must* have high cards to stay in without a pair or three in sequence or three to a flush.

6. Call. This is one of the stronger optional calls listed earlier in this chapter. (See page 66 for your chance of developing kings over or better in a situation almost identical to this.)

7. I advise folding this type of hand, but if you have just bagged a big one and the adrenalin is active, toss in a dime. If you don't improve on the next card, be sure to drop. Do you announce "I'll see one more" on this type of hand? If you do, be

sure you also announce "I'll see just one more" when you start
with three of a kind wired.

8. Call, but this is not as good as it looks. Remember that two
low pairs can be nasty.

9. Your chance of winning is very strong. Should you raise? Not
yet. Not in second position. You'll drive out players with
little chance of beating you.

10. A sound call.

Now make one change in the conditions. Raise the ante to 30
cents. It is not the fact that *you* put in 30 cents that's important.
What is important is that there is $2.10 in the pot, so the bal-
ancing of your chance of winning and the odds you receive from
this point on are different than with a 10-cent ante. Do any of
your decisions change? Well, the hands you called are certainly
unchanged. Hands 1 and 7 look a little better. If there isn't much
raising on the first card in your game you might as well call.
Hands 2, 3 and 5 are still too weak. Resist any temptation to
protect your ante. When you picked up these miserable cards
your portion of the $2.10 in the center of the table disappeared.
The $2.10 is still out on the table, but when you draw poor cards
your claim on any portion of the pot is gone.

Try another modification. Suppose the ante was $5. There is
$35 in the pot. The guy to your right boldly bets 10 cents. The
pot is tremendous and you call on all ten hands.

We can now play around with the first hand for a while. Remember that I folded this one for a 10-cent ante, but let's ana-
lyze some further developments. You hold:

K♡ 9♠ 8♡   Exposed cards are: K♠ 2♡ Q♣ J♢
                                     5♡ 4♢

You draw as your fourth card each of the following:

    5♣   Fold if a bet is made
    3♣   Fold if a bet is made
    Q♢   Fold if a bet is made
    4♠   Fold if a bet is made
    7♣   Call if a bet is made
    3♡   Call if a bet is made

6♡   Call, of course. This is three to a flush and also has straight possibilities

9◇   Call

K◇   Your best draw. Call

6◇   This is a temptation only if no 7s are exposed on this round. Did you have a good day? Then see one more. I fold.

J♣   This is a little better. It's better because the card is higher and the straight will be higher. If you are playing tight, you should fold this one too.

Try a fifth card? There sure are lots of combinations. I asked my mathematician friends how many there were for the first three cards. The answer was something like this: 52 things taken 3 at a time is 52 x 51 x 50 divided by 3 times 2 times 1. There are about 22,000 combinations and many, many more to come on later cards. There are around 134,000,000 possible seven-card hands in a deck of 52 cards. You have an equal chance of getting any one of them. It's a fascinating game. Most of the possible hands are terrible. Four of them are royal flushes and are certain winners. Each of the others must be weighed against the possible holding of your opponents. If you draw a full house, you might lose to a higher full house. The next pot can be won by a pair of aces. It can be most distressing.

There has been no raising. At the fifth card there are three players. The pot amounts to $1.70.

	Down		Up		
You	K♡	9♠	8♡	9◇	7◇
Opponent	?	?	K♠	J♣	5♠
Dealer	?	?	4◇	7♣	J♡

Other exposed cards were: 2♡ Q♣ J◇ 5♡ 6♠.

You survey the board. What did Dealer stay on to start with? He might be seeking a straight, or does he have a high pair in the hole? Opponent's hand is deceptive. As you are thinking about his possible hole cards, he checks. Dealer bets 30 cents.

You consider folding, but call painfully; should have dropped out at the start. Opponent also calls.

On the sixth card you draw the 9 of clubs. This is your best possible draw. You get a warm feeling. Poker isn't so bad after all, you muse. You drag comfortably on your cigarette. Opponent draws the 4 of hearts. Dealer gets an ace. You bet 30 cents on your three 9s. Opponent turns his cards. Dealer raises to 60 cents. Should you reraise? Study Dealer's cards. Review the cards that were turned. Were any clubs turned? There certainly were. Not a single ace has been exposed except the one Dealer just received! Do you still want to raise? Your final card doesn't help. You check. Dealer bets. You call. Dealer turns up a pair of aces in the hole!

Three 9s is a good hand in seven-card stud, but it doesn't always win. Ability at the poker table is divided into two departments. The more important and easier to master is the technical. It concerns the need to evaluate your chance of developing the highest hand compared with the payoff when you do succeed, and the chance of failure to hold the highest hand and the cost when you hold a loser. A proper evaluation requires that you use all the available information, especially the exposed cards. You must, therefore, get into the habit of remembering cards that have been turned. You must also learn to use this information in your evaluation. It works two ways. You use the information in judging your possibility of improving your own hand. You also use the knowledge of exposed cards in judging the strength of your opponent's hand.

I mentioned two departments, one being mastery of the technical problems. The other lies in the whole area of deception. Let's stay in the technical department for a while.

Can you estimate the chance of winning, the cost of trying and the odds you get? Here is a condensation from the pages of a book on poker dealing with a simple problem:

> *The game is five-card stud. One player holds a spade in the hole and three spades up. The spades are all small cards. The*

opponent holds two kings exposed and a side card. There are
36 unexposed cards. Six of them are spades. The odds are 5
to 1 against drawing a spade. There are 11 chips in the pot.
Kings bet two chips—the limit. If the four flush calls there are
15 chips in the pot. Assume the flush makes and that kings
will check. Flush will bet two chips, the limit, and kings will
call. The total of the pot is 19 chips. Four were invested by
the player seeking the flush. The odds received were 15 to 4—
about 4 to 1. His chance of making the flush was 5 to 1. His
search for the flush in five-card stud was a bad risk.*

Was this author's analysis correct? I think not. Was the
mythical and supposedly inept player who stayed on the flush
taking the correct action? Yes. Most poker players would stay in
this situation and they would be correct. Let's study the situation
more carefully. Consider not only the pot in which the flush is
made but also some others. In six hands with all conditions
identical, a spade should come up once and fail to come up

* Steig, *Poker for Fun and Profit*, op. cit., p. 78.

five times. The five hands where the flush is not made will
cost ten chips, as you will not call the final bet after the fifth
card. When you make the flush you will win 15 chips. If the kings
do not call your final bet you will win only 13. In either case
you show a profit on the six hands taken as one unit. In Appen-
dix C the precise computation of this problem is given. If you
can stand the arithmetic, study the solution. It will give you
some insight into similar situations.

Let me caution you that I am not advising as a general rule
to draw to a four flush in five-card stud. Under the conditions
stated above, it was the proper play. Modify the conditions by
raising the two chips bet to five chips and it is a losing proposition. The five pots you lose when the flush doesn't come in will
cost 25 chips. You can't recover that much in the hands you win.
Reduce the 11 chips in the pot, and it may also be a losing
proposition.

So in a very simple five-card-stud situation, with loads of time
to do the arithmetic, it wasn't done properly. Can you estimate
your chances accurately at the table in a complex game like
seven-card stud? It's impossible. But your opponents can't estimate their situation either.

You can remember the cards that were folded, learn a little
about probabilities, have a general notion of the size of the pot
and use this information intelligently. You must not only consider your chances of improving but also your opponents'
chances of improving. Here is an extreme illustration:

	Down		Up			
You	5♡	A♡	10♠	5◊	7♡	A♠
A	?	?	10♡	2♡	10♣	3♡
B	?	?	K♡	7◊	6♡	7♣
C	?	?	6◊	8♡	7♠	9♡

Cards folded earlier by others included a K, 10, 5, 5, Q♡, 4♡.
There has been no raising on any of the earlier rounds to suggest
strength. Consider each of the opponents' prospects. C has no

chance for a straight; all the 5s and 10s are out. C thinks a 5 is live but you have it in the hole. Look at B. His 7s are dead and a king and 6 are also dead. A's hearts are dead, considering your two in the hole which he doesn't know about. Tens are also dead.

A bets his 10s confidently. B and C call. You should raise. The cards that have been closed and your concealed cards reduce the chances of all your opponents. True, any of your opponents could make a full house. But your prospects of winning are very strong. You raise to try to build the pot. You might even make a full house, as your aces are live.

In problem eight on page 35 you started with a pair of 9s and stayed for the first bet. Give your answer to each of the six problems below before you read the discussion.

	Down		Up	
Lucky			K♠	7♡
You	9◊	9♣	6♠	
Clown			2♡	2◊
Dealer			Q♣	9♠

Other exposed cards of players who dropped on the first bet are: J◊, 5♡, 4◊. There is $1.10 in the pot. Clown bets 20 cents; Dealer and Lucky call.

What is your action with each of the following cards:

1.	3♡	4.	9♡
2.	Q♠	5.	K♣
3.	A◊	6.	7♣

Comments:

1. Fold. The exposed 9 of spades hurts this hand.
2. Fold. One demerit for calling.
3. Call
4. Don't you dare raise. It is too early.
5. Optional
6. Call because no 8s are exposed

Make this change. You sit between Clown and Dealer and must act before you know what Dealer and Lucky will do. All holdings are identical. You now get two demerits on number 2 because of the danger of a raise in back of you. A raise on 4, while not recommended when you were last, is a tragedy in second position. You might kill a juicy situation. Five is now a doubtful call and 6 becomes optional.

With the positions as originally indicated, assume that Lucky raises to 40 cents. Fold 1, 2, 5 and 6. You have lost only 20 cents. Drink a beer and observe. Call the raise on 4. Three is optional. The decision depends on what you know about Lucky and how your own luck is running.

Assume Lucky did not raise and the next card is dealt. Six more problems are listed below. Compare your answer with the comments given later.

	Down		Up		
Lucky			K♠	7♡	2♣
You	9◇	9♣	6♠	A◇	
Clown			2♡	2◇	6◇
Dealer			Q♣	9♠	Q♡

You draw K♣. What is your action on problems 1 and 2?

1. Dealer bets 30 cents. Lucky calls.
2. Dealer bets 30 cents. Lucky raises to 60 cents.
   You draw 6♡ for two pair.
3. Dealer bets 30 cents. Lucky calls.
4. Dealer bets 30 cents. Lucky raises.
   You draw 9♡
5. Dealer bets 30 cents. Lucky calls.
   You draw A♣
6. You bet 30 cents. Clown folds. Dealer calls. Lucky raises.

1. Call
2. Fold. You have only lost 40 cents in this pot. Even if you buy well you may not win.
3. Call

4. Fold. You must improve to win this pot.
5. It's time to raise
6. Lucky probably has three of a kind, but you'll have to sweat this one out. Check on the next card if you don't improve.

Assume there was no raising on the previous round.

	Down		*Up*			
Lucky			K♠	7♡	2♣	7♠
You	9♢	9♣	6♠	A♢	K♣	
Clown			2♡	2♢	6♢	4♡
Dealer			Q♣	9♠	Q♡	10♢

You get the 9♡. What is your action in each of these situations?
1. Dealer bets 30 cents. Lucky calls.
2. Dealer bets 30 cents. Lucky raises.
   6♣ is dealt to you. What do you do in the circumstances described?
3. Dealer bets 30 cents. Lucky calls.
4. Dealer bets 30 cents. Lucky raises.
5. Dealer bets 30 cents. Lucky calls. You call. Clown raises. Dealer calls. Lucky calls.
6. Dealer bets 30 cents. Lucky calls. You call. Clown raises. Dealer raises to 90. Lucky drops.

1. Raise
2. Raise or call is optional. Depends very heavily on the type of game and your evaluation of the players.
3. Call
4. Fold. It's too expensive. Only two cards can help.
5. Call. This is a close decision. Clown can have a straight, three deuces or a small full house. If you pull a 9 or a 6, you'll beat any of these. It costs only 30 cents more to try. There is about $5 in the pot. If you fail to improve, you fold. If you improve, you'll probably win $5 or more for a 30-cent risk. The total of the pot will depend on the last

round of betting. Your chance of making a full house is 14½ to 1.* You are getting better odds than that.

6. Two new factors exist. You must pay 60 cents. The odds you get are greatly reduced and well below 14½ to 1 which is your chance of improving. Second, you may draw the full house and be beaten. Dealer looks like a straight, but he might be better and his full house will be higher than yours. Get your tail out of this pot.

The final bet in seven-card stud is usually easy. The pot is so big ordinarily that you call if there is any reasonable hope of winning for a 30-cent bet. If there is a raise, it isn't so clear-cut. You have to take a view on two pair.

These are some typical situations faced over and over again in a small-stakes game. They have been analyzed in terms of a liberal style of play for money that counts but won't send you to the poorhouse. You may have to adjust a little for your own game. If you play for bigger stakes, where you can get hurt badly in an evening's play, greater caution must be exercised, especially for the first and second bet. If you get out early on poor cards, you'll avoid the nasty middle-round problems.

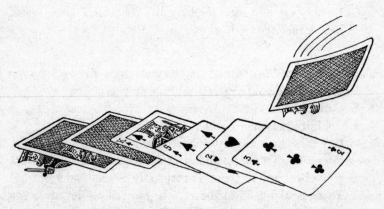

* You now see 18 cards. Three were folded earlier. There are 31 unexposed cards which still include one 6 and one 9.

3

Meet
Freddie

Who is Freddie? He plays in your poker game every week. See
if you recognize him: He is a successful attorney during business hours. He is happily married and has two fine kids. Freddie
is a pillar of your community. He is the assistant cubmaster of
the pack in the neighborhood. He is active in the P.T.A. When
your lawnmower breaks down, it is Freddie who comes to the
rescue. On Friday nights he comes to relax at the poker table,
and this articulate, soft-spoken, kindly and intelligent character
goes through a metamorphosis. It starts slowly, but in about a
half hour or so Mr. Freddie "Hyde" emerges. He babbles. He
misdeals. He calls or raises out of turn when he has a good hand.
At other times he is in a trance. When it comes his turn he
asks, "What's the bet?" or "Who raised?" When he has his flush
or straight, he scarcely glances at his last card. When he needs
to improve on his last card, he carefully inserts it between his
other two hole cards and squeezes the spots off it. If the last
card helps, he immediately drops his cards, looks around and
asks, "Who is high?" Every now and again he realizes some
deception is part of the game, but he is a poor actor and gives
it away. When he takes an action he knows is bad he announces,
"I came to gamble." Let's play a few hands of seven-card stud
with Freddie.

Conditions of the game: 10-cent ante, 10 cents first bet, 20 cents second and third bets, and 30 cents on last two bets. Open pair on second and third up cards also may bet 30 cents; no sandbagging.

	Down	Up
Frank		3♡
Fred	K♡ J◇	10♣
Bill		A♠
Paul		4♡
Al		7◇
Herb		8♡
Jim		K◇

Fred loves this hand. (Note the huge cigar instead of the usual cigarette.) It's worth playing, but is not nearly so good as he would like to believe.

> Bill is high and bets 10 cents
> Paul calls
> Al folds
> Herb calls
> Jim folds
> Frank folds
> Freddie calls. He thought of raising but resisted the temptation. Freddie announces, "This will be an interesting hand."

2nd up card

	Down		Up	
Fred	J♦ K♡		10♣	5♣
Bill			A♠	4♣
Paul			4♡	9♡
Herb			8♡	Q♡

Fred is beginning to lose interest.

Bill checks
Paul checks
Herb bets 20 cents
Fred is deep in thought. He looks around and realizes it is
    his turn. He calls.
Bill calls
Paul calls

5th card

	Down		Up		
Fred	J♦ K♡		10♣	5♣	K♠
Bill			A♠	4♣	4♠
Paul			4♡	9♡	9♦
Herb			8♡	Q♡	K♣

Fred is interested again. He so wanted a queen that at first he
was displeased. Now his blood is racing again. "Who's high?"
he asks. Al, who is out of the hand, twists his toothpick. He
knows the king helped and probably paired him. Al also notes
that the 5 and 10 are live. Even the folded cards didn't show a
5 or 10. Two pair, kings over, could win this one. Freddie is
oblivious to this kind of analysis. He rarely looks at the exposed
cards. He never remembers those turned in the early play. He
tries every now and then, but gives it up.

Paul is high and bets 30 cents
All others call

6th card

	Down		Up			
Fred	J◊	K♡	10♣	5♣	K♠	5♡
Bill			A♠	4♣	4♠	5◊
Paul			4♡	9♡	9◊	7♣
Herb			8♡	Q♡	K♣	3◊

Freddie is really interested now.

Paul bets 30 cents
Herb calls
Freddie raises to 60 cents. "Let's separate the men from the boys." Al winces.
All players call the raise

7th card

	Down		Up				Down
Fred	J◊	K♡	10♣	5♣	K♠	5♡	7♠
Bill			A♠	4♣	4♠	5◊	
Paul			4♡	9♡	9◊	7♣	
Herb			8♡	Q♡	K♣	3◊	

Paul checks
Herb checks
Freddie bets 30 cents
Bill raises to 60 cents
Paul and Herb drop
Freddie studies the situation. He frowns. He calls the raise.

"Kings over," Fred announces. Bill turns a 6, 7, 8. "Small straight." Bill rakes in the chips. Al sips his beer. Freddie lights a cigarette. "I had to play that one." Bill stacks his chips neatly.

Fred lost a tough one. Surprisingly enough, he made no mistakes on the first hand. His costly mistakes are staying when he should drop and failing to capitalize on his winning hands. As the previous hand presented no difficult technical problems, he made no mistakes. A cautious player might drop after the second up card, but it is close and depends on the type of game.

The players in the game like Fred, although some of them won't admit it. He doesn't mean to bet out of turn. When he does, and it hurts one of the players, it is philosophical to figure that he helps by such actions other times, so it balances in the long run. In fact, in the long run only Fred is hurt.

Al is particularly fond of Freddie. Not because Fred pays for those expensive suits Al treasures, or because he has compassion for the underdog. He just likes him as a person. Fred is a good friend; he is good company. Al has tried to teach him; Fred listens. It helps for a short while and then Fred slips back into his old habits.

	Down		Up
Fred	Q♡	Q♠	6◇
Bill			9♣
Paul			10♡
Al			J♠
Herb			4◇
Jim			K♣
Frank			8♠

Jim is high and bets 10 cents
Frank folds
Fred calls
Bill folds
Paul calls
Al calls
Herb folds

4th card

	Down		Up		
Fred	Q♡	Q♠	6◇	Q♣	Fred pulls a "goodie"
Paul			10♡	9◇	
Al			J♠	A♡	
Jim			K♣	5♠	

Freddie beams. He bets 30 cents. A chorus descends on him. "You're not high, and, besides, there is no open pair."

Al, who has jacks and was going to bet, checks
Jim checks
Freddie bets 20 cents
Paul folds
Al folds
Jim calls

Neither Jim nor Fred improved on the succeeding three cards. After each card Jim checked, Fred bet and Jim called. Jim had kings over. Freddie raked in the chips.

This hand came up next:

	Down		Up
Bill			J◇
Paul			A♣
Al			7♠
Herb			5♣
Jim			3◇
Frank			10♠
Fred	J♣	9♠	6♡

Freddie, glowing about the previous pot, plays this dog. Paul bets 10 cents. Fred and three others call. Freddie's next card is the 5 of spades. He stays for 20 cents. He draws the 2 of hearts for his fifth card. A 30-cent bet on an open pair had been raised to 60 cents by the time it reached Freddie. He ponders this a while and finally decides that his J♣, 9♠, 6♡, 5♠ and 2♡ doesn't offer much play. At this point in the play the three surviving players have (1) a flush, (2) aces over, and (3) three of a kind.

It didn't occur to Freddie that he should have conceded the 10-cent ante and dropped on the first bet. The persistent optimist, Freddie stays on anything after he wins a pot on the grounds that it might be the beginning of a lucky streak. He is right. It might be the beginning of a lucky streak. His next three cards might well be A♣, A♠, A♡. The lucky streak is over when his next three cards are J, 9, 6 of assorted suits.

The next hand was dealt, and this is what Freddie, still flushed with his earlier victory, saw:

	Down		Up
Paul			K♢
Al			A♣
Herb			7♢
Jim			6♠
Frank			10♢
Fred	5♢	A♠	5♡
Bill			A♢

Fred is pleased with his holding! With two aces exposed, it is nothing to be excited about.

> Al bets 10 cents
> Herb calls
> Jim and Frank fold
> Fred, Bill and Paul call

On the next card a five-spot is exposed. Now Freddie, who drew a 6, should certainly drop. His prospects of developing three 5s or aces over 5s are dreadful. Fourteen cards have been exposed. There are thirty-eight unknown cards of which only two are an ace or 5.

Fred plays on to the bitter end. On the seventh card he draws another small pair. The pot is won by kings over!

Fred next saw this hand:

	Down		*Up*
Al			J♡
Herb			4♡
Jim			K♠
Frank			6♡
Fred	Q◊	J♣	9♣
Bill			9♠
Paul			2◊

Jim bets 10 cents. Frank, Fred and Al call.

4th card

	Down		*Up*	
Al			J♡	7♡
Jim			K♠	A◊
Frank			6♡	9◊
Fred	Q◊	J♣	9♣	10♣

Fred's prospects are bright. He has a better than even chance of making the straight at this point with only one of his straight cards exposed. His chance of straighting is very close to four out of seven. Fred considers raising. He wants to sweeten the pot. Jim bets and when it comes Fred's turn he has reached no conclusion. He calls. Fred's next card is the 3◊. Al bets 30 cents with a pair of 7s. Jim bumps it to 60 cents. Fred, who was still wondering about raising before the betting started, is now relieved of the problem and merely calls. Frank drops. Freddie now draws the 3 of clubs, giving him a pair of 3s. He frowns. Al checks. Jim bets. Fred and Al call.

Fred's final card is the ace of clubs. Fred is annoyed. He started with an excellent draw to a straight. It hasn't come in. Here is Freddie's hand: Q◇ J♣ 9♣ 10♣ 3◇ 3♣ A♣.

Al checks and Jim bets 30 cents. Fred starts to fold. He looks at his hand once more, with a startled double-take. He has drawn a flush! Fred raises. Al drops. Jim calls.

Freddie wins a big pot!

On the next hand Fred draws 10, 8, 6. He stays and gets a 7. One 9 is exposed. His lucky streak might materialize. He is already ahead for the night, and another win will sweeten it. Fred stays all the way, trying for an inside straight, and doesn't make it.

The pot cost him close to $2, as a pair showed early and there was a raise to 60 cents on one of the bets.

Was Freddie lucky or unlucky? Actually he drew better than average cards, so in that sense he was certainly lucky. He won one large pot and one small one out of six. He played three of his losing pots all the way and dropped early in the remaining hand. He ended up about even. This was one of his better sessions. Imagine the results when he draws poorly.

Let's experiment. Assume Al played Fred's cards in the preceding six hands and see what happens.

Hand 1: Al would stay to the first card on K♡, J♢, 10♣. In fact he would play it all the way, just as Fred had.

Hand 2: Al, of course, would win a big one. He never bets out of turn. He never bets an incorrect amount. He has a fine feel for the table. On the fourth card the ace high would bet. Jim would call or raise with kings over. Al would start to fold and then "stay for one more." His buddies know he is an actor, but they get confused anyway. He would raise later.

Hand 3: On J♣, 9♠, 6♡, he would drop and go for a pastrami sandwich.

Hand 4: Al would fold immediately and top the sandwich with a can of beer.

Hand 5: Al would probably raise on the four straight and maybe raise on subsequent rounds. He would win a bigger pot.

Hand 6: He would fold 10, 8, 6 and observe.

Summing up, Al would lose three 10-cent antes and one expensive pot; he would win two big ones. When he draws good cards, he wins. He sometimes wins when he draws poor cards. And when he wins, he wins big; his losses are usually small.

4

The Elusive
Lady

Over the course of the last year or two, has your poker action
added up to a plus or a minus result? Now, I don't mean the
results you admit publicly. I'm talking about the results without
rounding your wins up and your losses down and with no
omissions because it wasn't your regular game or for other
reasons you may contrive. Over a long run of 300 or 400 hours of
poker, if your result is on the minus side you are playing losing
poker. It isn't luck. You are being outplayed.

In 400 hours you play about 5,000 hands of seven-card stud.
In a sequence of that length the chance that you drew significantly poorer cards than your opponents is trivial. It is certainly
possible, in fact probable, that you will draw poor cards for
several hours, but over that 5,000-hand stretch the bad sequences will almost surely have been balanced by equally good
sequences. And in any run of several thousand hands the result
will be close to an even balance between good and poor cards.

Let me tell you about the summer of 1954. I had been playing
in a quarter-and-a-half, dealer's-choice game for a couple of
years. High-low games were played all the time. Occasionally a
player dealt a dull hand of draw or five-card stud, but only for

the purpose of being cute. The games played were rather wild for the most part, so that quarter-and-a-half stakes resulted in some consequential swings. A loss or win below $25 was small. A swing of $25 to $50 was fair-sized. A swing from $50 to $75 was big. Over $75 occurred only rarely.

I had been winning in pretty good style for a two-year period. Along came a Friday night in June when I lost $35. Two weeks later we had our next session. I lost $56. Two weeks later . . . It's painful even now. I lost amounts ranging from $35 to $67 for seven consecutive sessions. It added up to about $300.

What I had to say about probabilities and luck balancing in the long run could also fill a book. This was the longest sustained losing streak I ever experienced in years of poker, as well as other forms of gambling. Each of the losses was on the heavy side. And it happened in a game where I thought I had a decided edge.

It was a long, hot, miserable summer. Toward the end of the summer I arrived at the game like a punch-drunk fighter—ready for action but defeated before the first card was dealt. I played very cautiously, but nothing helped. I drew badly. When I did get a card I needed, someone else drew even better. My strategy actions failed dismally. Nothing seemed to help. My morale at the table was shot. I also visited the Credit Union at work.

Then my luck changed suddenly and sharply. I won all of it back plus a little more in four remarkable sessions. I had one win of $99 in a game where $70 or $75 was a rare event. I couldn't go wrong. If I needed a heart, it came along. If I needed to draw a 6 to make a perfect low, it came in. Everyone stayed against my good hands, sweetening the pot. If I had a high-looking hand and bet strongly as a bluff, the high players folded or declared low.

Is there a point to this? There is. The laws of chance or probability which predict that good and bad hands will be dealt to you about evenly in a long run also tell us that winning and losing streaks can and should occur. In fact, the chance (or odds) that a losing streak of particular length will occur can be computed. Fortunately, poker is a game of skill, and when you do hit a long losing streak a skillful player minimizes his losses. Imagine what happens to the inept player!

You may continue to gripe and slam the cards on the table when you are losing. This is a privilege which belongs to losers. If you think Lady Luck is frowning on you in particular, you're

wrong. It is all part of a grand pattern that can be called the laws of chance or the laws of probability. In some situations it is easy to figure out the chance of a particular series of events occurring. In other situations, it requires an expert with vast resources at his command.

Let's make a minor digression and deal with dice as a simple exercise in probabilities. If you have no interest in this, just skip the next few paragraphs. There is no skill at all in the tossing of honest dice, and the information which follows can be used to compute the result of almost any dice problem.

If a die is perfect, its chance of coming to rest on a particular side is one in six. In tossing a pair of dice, there are 36 (6 x 6) possible combinations. Each single combination has an equal chance of coming up on each toss. The odds against a particular combination are 35 to 1. Here is our problem. Is it an even bet that the dice will pass? Study the following table.

(1) All Combinations	(2) Value	(3) No. of Combs. for the Value	(4) Odds Against	(5) Pass		(6) Don't Pass	
1-1	2	1	35 to 1				1
1-2, 2-1	3	2	17 to 1				2
3-1, 1-3, 2-2	4	3	11 to 1	1			2
2-3, 3-2, 4-1, 1-4	5	4	8 to 1	8/5	(1.60)	12/5	(2.40)
1-5, 5-1, 4-2, 2-4, 3-3	6	5	31 to 5	25/11	(2.27)	30/11	(2.73)
1-6, 6-1, 5-2, 2-5, 4-3, 3-4	7	6	5 to 1	6			
2-6, 6-2, 3-5, 5-3, 4-4	8	5	31 to 5	25/11	(2.27)	30/11	(2.73)
3-6, 6-3, 5-4, 4-5	9	4	8 to 1	8/5	(1.60)	12/5	(2.40)
4-6, 6-4, 5-5	10	3	11 to 1	1			2
6-5, 5-6	11	2	17 to 1	2			
6-6	12	1	35 to 1				1
Total		36		17.74		18.26	

The 36 possible combinations of a pair of dice are all listed in the first column. They are grouped according to the results that have a meaning in a dice game. These results, the total value, are shown in the second column. The third column is the count of the number of combinations in the first column that yield the value in the second column. There are four combinations that make a five, six combinations that make a seven, and so on. Remember that each of the 36 combinations has an equal chance of occurring.

The fourth column gives the true odds for one roll of the dice. It is 11 to 1 that you don't throw a four; it is 5 to 1 that you don't throw a seven; etc. In a Nevada casino, if you bet on the Field Numbers, you have 2, 3, 4, 9, 10, 11, 12. The house has 5, 6, 7, 8. You have seven numbers and the house has only four. Consider, however, the number of combinations. The house has twenty. You have sixteen. You bet even money when you should be getting 5-to-4 odds. Every nine times you bet a dollar on the "Field" you should have a net loss of $1.

In the fifth and sixth columns we have assigned the Pass and Don't Pass values. We shall study the problem in terms of the 36 sets of combinations. In dice, 7 or 11 on the first roll win immediately. Since 7 should come up six times out of 36 rolls, we enter 6 in the Pass column. Eleven comes up twice in 36, so we enter 2 in the Pass column. Don't Pass, get the 2, 3, 12 on the first roll. If a 4, 5, 6, 8, 9 or 10 comes up on your first roll, that number is your point. On succeeding rolls, if your point comes up before a 7, you win. If a 7 comes up before your point, you lose.

Let's review these prospects. A 4 has three combinations. A 7 has six combinations. Each of these combinations has an equal chance of coming up. So the odds are 2 to 1 against passing. In three chances, you should pass once and lose twice. So we enter 1 in the Pass column and 2 in the Don't Pass column. The odds are 3 to 2 against a 5 coming up before a 7. The dice should pass two out of five. However, as 5 came up only four times in our initial set of 36, the number of winners is 4 x 2/5 or 8/5. The rest of columns 5 and 6 are filled out by the same type of arithmetic. The fractions convert to decimals as indicated in the parentheses.

The answer to our problem is obtained by adding up the values in columns 5 and 6. The result can be described in various ways, but in any way it means that honest dice will pass less often than they will not pass. Here is the simplest way of describing the result. The odds are approximately 1.03 to 1 against the dice passing. A mathematician would say that the probability the dice will pass is .493.

In poker the odds in particular situations are much harder to figure, as there are thousands of combinations. In some situations there are millions of combinations. Most of the draw-poker problems where you would like to know the chance of drawing a particular hand are easy. As in dice, they have been computed and appear in various forms in books covering this game.* In seven-card stud it is much harder. Every time a card is exposed, the odds on improving your hand change. You can't possibly commit the odds on all the pertinent situations to memory. Nor do you have the time or inclination to compute them at the table. Furthermore, there is more than probability theory involved. You must also determine the odds you are getting. In addition, you are facing real live opponents, and their characteristics and style must never be ignored. Rumor has it that Herb is fiddling around with his secretary. This will probably affect his poker game but in an indeterminate way. That's what makes poker such a fascinating game.

Here are the odds for a few common situations. We'll go through the computations so that you will see how it is done. You hold five cards of which four are spades. There are four opponents still playing, so you see their twelve exposed cards (three per player). Two other players dropped at the first card. There are nineteen exposed cards—five of yours and fourteen of your opponents'. You see three spades in your opponents' cards. One spade was folded earlier. There are five remaining spades.

* The most comprehensive work on poker probabilities will be found in Oswald Jacoby, *How to Figure the Odds,* Doubleday and Co., Inc., 1947, and *Oswald Jacoby on Poker,* Doubleday, 1947.

There are 33 cards unexposed. These include the cards in the deck and down cards of all other players. You are to receive two more cards of 33. A list of all possible two-card combinations could be made, and then we could count the number which would give you a flush. This count divided by the total number of combinations listed would give the probability or chance of making a flush. There are shorter ways of accomplishing this. In this case, the easiest way is to figure out the probability of not making the flush. There are five spades out of 33 remaining. The chance that your sixth card will not be a flush card is 28 out of 33 and your seventh card will not be a spade 27 chances out of 32. The solution is: $28/33 \times 27/32 = 756/1056 = .716$. This is the probability of not getting a flush. The chance of making the flush is .284. Roughly the odds are 2½ to 1 against your making the flush.

In the first four cards you hold two pair—6s and 7s. Compute the chance of making a full house or four of a kind. No 6 or 7 shows in any of the cards exposed in the hands of your opponents. Counting your four cards and the exposed cards of your opponents, there are 14 exposed cards and 38 unexposed. Four of the latter are 6s and 7s. Again it is easier to do it backward. Compute as follows: $34/38 \times 33/37 \times 32/36 = \dfrac{35,904}{50,616} =$ .709. This is the chance of not making the full house or four of a kind. The chance of making the full house with three more draws is about .291. We have failed to take one fact into account. The card you draw as your fifth card could be paired on the sixth and drawn again on the seventh. This is another way to make a full house when your first four cards are two pair. As this is a very remote possibility, we will merely round our result up a trifle to .30 and call that the answer. In simpler terms, the odds are 7 to 3 against making a full house or better.

If a 6 or 7 is exposed in the "up" cards of one of your opponents, compute it as follows: $35/38 \times 34/37 \times 33/36 = \dfrac{39,270}{50,616} =$ .776 (answer against). Making four of a kind or full house is

.224. Round up to .230 to allow for the fifth, sixth and seventh as the same card. Odds are about 3½ to 1 against making a full house or better.

Enough arithmetic. You can't do it at the table. To help you evaluate your possibilities, we have computed the probabilities for some key situations that occur frequently. You'll find them in an addendum to this chapter.

Part of the judgment of your play must also be your guess of the odds you are getting in a situation. You can't figure that out, obviously. As a rough guide, make a note of what the pots usually come to in your game over the course of a few weeks of play. Remember this: in many situations you will not have to call the last bet if you don't make the hand you are seeking. Suppose a game usually yields a pot between $5 and $6 and this looks as if it will be an average pot. You are betting after five cards. It will cost you 30 cents to see the sixth card and 30 cents to see the seventh card. If you don't make the flush you are seeking, you can fold without calling the bet after the seventh card. In our first calculation, you are getting odds of about 4.50 to .60 or 7½ to 1. Knock it down to 6 to 1 on the grounds that you might lose even if you make the flush. If someone looks really strong, consider it 5 to 1. If you expect some raising so that it will cost more than 60 cents to get the sixth and seventh card, you have to reduce the odds given above. We noted earlier a particular problem of making a flush with two draws remaining where there were five spades left unexposed. In that instance the odds were 2½ to 1 against making the flush. In short, in this typical situation, a four flush in five cards, you get better than 4 to 1 in money odds on a 2½ to 1 chance of making the flush. If you could gamble with this one situation over and over again for hours, you would be a big winner.

Remember also that the odds change every time a card is exposed. If you start with a four flush in diamonds in the first four cards and on the fifth card you don't hit, but two or three diamonds are drawn by your opponents, your prospects have deteriorated.

It is most important that you watch all the exposed cards. Remember the exposed cards that have been turned. This cannot be stressed enough. Just a few nights before I started this chapter I sat in a game where a player in seven-card high-low stayed for the sixth and seventh cards seeking a 9 for an inside straight. Two 9s were on the table. Two had been folded.

So forget about luck. Gripe when you're losing. It makes a good show. Concentrate on getting the most out of your cards. You'll get your share of good hands and, if you handle them properly, you'll win big.

Addendum to Chapter 4

We covered a flush-probability problem earlier in this chapter. (This is also a solution for a straight where the same number of unexposed cards are available to make the straight.) We shall study some ordinary two-pair and three-of-a-kind problems. Get a feel for these results without necessarily memorizing them. The game is seven-card stud.

1. If your first three cards in seven-card stud are 7♠, 7♡, K◇, there are six opponents, and *none* of their exposed cards is a 7 or K:

    Your chance of pulling two pair with kings over or better is somewhat more than: **40 chances in 100**

    The odds are a little better than: **3 to 2 against**

    Please note that kings over and three 7s are most of the 40 positive results with a full house being a very small portion.

    Summary: If you start with a small pair and an ace or king kicker and *none* of your cards is exposed, you have a good solid gamble going for you.

2. Consider the same problem as above, but now assume that one K *and* one 7 are exposed.

    Where your prospects of ending with kings over or better were more than 40 in 100, they decline to about: **25 chances in 100 or 3 to 1 against**

    Summary: This is a very sharp reduction in your chances of winning the hand compared with 1. above. It should be particularly noted that your chance of three 7s or better has dropped even more sharply.

3. Suppose you hold 7♠, 7♡, 2♣ and *none* of these is exposed in opponents' up cards.

    Your chance of making three 7s or better is: **18 in 100 or 4½ to 1 against**

Your *additional* chance of pulling aces
or kings to make aces or kings over is: 7½ in 100
The combination of these, for kings
over or better, comes to about: 25 in 100
                                                           or 3 to 1 against

Summary: 7, 7, 2 is a poor start compared
with 7, 7, A or 7, 7, K.

4. You start with A, K, 7 of assorted suits
   and *none* of these cards is exposed in
   your opponents' hands.

   Your chance of making kings over or
   better (disregarding straight or flush
   possibilities) is: 24 in 100
                                                           or about 3 to 1
                                                           against

   Summary: This gives you a decent gamble in a game that isn't too tight. It is the
   best of the optional calls in the second
   chapter. Note that it yields the same result as 3. above for kings over or better.
   But 3. is listed as a good start (not optional) in Chapter 2 because the chance
   of getting three of a kind on 7, 7, 2 is considerably better than three of a kind on
   A, K, 7.

5. Assume you hold A, K, 7, 7, 9 (with no
   flush possibility) after five cards have
   been dealt. There are 15 exposed cards
   in the hands of your opponents, including those folded.

   a. Assume the exposed cards include one
      ace, one king, but no 7s or 9s.

      Your prospects of making kings over
      or better with the sixth and seventh
      card are: 35 chances in 100
      which is 13 to 7 or: about 2 to 1 against

Summary: This gives you a pretty good gamble if there is no exceptionally strong hand showing, because the money odds you get *at this point* are usually considerably higher than 2 to 1.

b. Assume two aces, one king, one 7 but no 9s are exposed in opponents' cards.

Kings over or better is approximately:

which is:

25 chances in 100
3 to 1 against

6. Change your holding to A, 7, 7, 9, 4. You have switched the K for a 4. Now note the drop in your prospects.

As before, 15 cards are exposed by your opponents, leaving 32 unexposed.

a. Assume one ace, one king, no 9s, no 7s and no 4s were exposed (similar to 5 a.).

You had 35 chances in 100 of kings over or better in 5 a. You now have:

25 chances in 100
or 3 to 1 against

b. Assume exposed cards are two aces, one king, one 7, no 9s, no 4s (similar to 5 b.).

Your prospects of kings over or better are very dim. They are:

14 chances in 100
or 6 to 1 against

5

Be a Chicken Plucker

Have you heard a poker player announce as he raises, "Let's get rid of the chicken pluckers" or "This will separate the men from the boys"? Well, sometimes you should be a chicken plucker. Of all the silly reasons for raising, this is the silliest. The very players you drive out are those least likely to win the pot. They are the players you should not want to knock out.

There are two reasons for raising. The more important one is that you think you have the best chance of winning the pot and you want it to be a big one. The second reason is when you raise as a deceptive or strategy play. Deceptive plays include bluffing, but they include far more. Such plays will be discussed in later chapters.

A study of when to raise is also a study of when not to raise. In either case the objective is the same. You are attempting to build the size of the pot when you expect to win or have excellent prospects of winning. You sometimes build the biggest pot by raising. In other situations, you build the biggest pot by not raising. The style of the game in which you participate is important in deciding when to raise. If it is a loose game, you should raise freely when you want to build a big pot. If it is a tight game,

you must be more cautious and hold back occasionally. Position at the table is also critical. If you must bet immediately after the high man on board, the risk of drop-outs behind you is increased. If you are in last position, you can raise rather freely, as the players are trapped between you and the high man.

When is a game tight and when is it loose? Here is a rough guide you can use. In a seven-hand game of seven-card stud, if six players are in most of the hands after the first bet when the ante is small, it is a very loose game. If four or five usually play, it is average or a little loose. If three play most of the pots, it is a tough group you play with. The standards given in Chapter 2 will generally result in three or four players after the first bet.

The next few times you play, make a point of watching the action after a raise. Generally raises in late rounds will drop few players in limit-stakes poker. You also have to consider the particular players. Weak players rarely drop after a raise. They hardly ever know what is going on anyway. Strong players pay careful attention to everything that happens at the table. They frequently fold if the betting gets stiff early in the hand.

Here is a pertinent anecdote. I arrived at Lae, New Guinea, in February 1944. The fighting in this area (except for some mopping up) was over and it became largely a supply base, staging area and headquarters for the 5th Air Force. Jungle warfare with all its hardships could be found some 25 miles away at Finschhafen.

Conversion of a fighting area to a behind-the-lines supply center meant different things to different people. It meant time for relaxation. It meant decent food occasionally. It meant good movies two or three times a week. Books became available. It usually brought a contingent or two of our fighting women, the WACS, WAFS, WAVES and so forth. The chase was on. It also meant time for furloughs and time for poker. After my first pay day in New Guinea, I found a poker game. It was a stiff game with stakes of one pound to five pounds (the Australian pound was worth $3.20). The game was almost always seven-card stud.

I played cautiously the first few hands. These were high stakes and I didn't know the players. It turned out to be a typical Army situation. The players for the most part acted as though each hand might be the last and they just couldn't bear sitting out of a pot. One of the players was even more emotional. He considered it a personal affront to be raised when he was high on the table. He always reraised. It didn't matter what he held; he reraised. Needless to say, a moderately decent run of cards was enough. I won a sizable sum. The game ended the next morning when our reraising friend went broke. Others had dropped out through the night, only to be replaced by equally eager GIs. It was a typical after-pay-day Army poker game.

The next evening I learned more about the reraising character. He was scheduled to leave on a furlough to Sydney, Australia, in a few days. He had been overseas for two years, mostly at different spots in New Guinea. He dropped close to 200 Australian pounds that he had been nursing at Port Moresby, at the battle of Buna, in the foxholes of Lae. A furlough, although supposedly a 30-day affair, usually came to almost 90 days because of the transportation problem. On the way back especially, a resourceful

GI could manage not to be around when transportation from Sydney to the Islands was available. A long stay in Sydney with normal designs required some folding money. So the winners put together a small stake for our benefactor and sent him to a well-deserved furlough.

This incident has come to mind many times in the years that have passed. I have often wondered how my poker-playing friend made out in Sydney. Also, whether he ever learned to control himself at the table.

In a seven-card-stud game, it is rarely good policy to raise on the first bet. It may be done occasionally but only if you are to the right of the high player or for some deceptive build-up. Almost never raise if you are to the left of the high man. In second position, the chance of driving out the other players is too great. Remember that your main purpose in raising is to build the pot when you have an excellent chance of winning.

The prospects for raising after the second up card are better. I do this occasionally, again when well placed at the table. Remember that once you raise, the other players will probably check to you on subsequent rounds. Frequently you get only one shot at raising for this reason. If four players are in for the second up card and you force two of them out, you end up reducing the size of the pot.

The fifth card (third up card) is the round for raising. This is particularly true if there is an open pair that bets the limit. You can then raise the limit. Raises on earlier rounds will frequently be too small to pay off. Another important practical point is that the typical game involves several poor players. A raise at the fifth card usually drops none of the weaker hands. They stay to protect their investment!

On the sixth and final card you raise freely. Build the biggest pot you possibly can, provided, of course, that you are sure to win the pot or have a fine prospect of winning.

An important feature in the art of proper raising is a good change of pace. This means that you must vary your action in standard situations just enough to keep your opponents guessing.

Otherwise they are more likely to drop against your raises. For example, you should normally raise on aces over after the fifth card with no unusual strength apparent. Maybe once or twice an evening you should raise holding a hand which might be aces over but isn't. When you do this it must be a situation where you have a good prospect of making a winner. Holding 8♠, K♡ down and 8♢, A♣, J♡ up, you ordinarily do not raise; but once in a while when your cards are very live, you should raise. You have reasonable prospects of winning, and the raise enlarges the pot. This type of play, made occasionally, protects those situations where you raise with a powerful holding.

An important problem is your ability to evaluate your prospects of winning. Aces over or better will usually win. I frequently raise on kings or queens over if the spot seems right. On two small pair, raising is not recommended. Relax and hope that you don't get raised. Your problem is not to build a big pot but to minimize your costs. You might even try folding two small pair if there is a raise. You'll find the results refreshing. When you do raise on two small pair, it is primarily for deceptive purposes.

You should raise with three of a kind unless there is some good reason to believe that you have stiff competition. Consider this problem:

	Down		Up			
			Q♡	7♠	9♣	7♢
Clown			Q♡	7♠	9♣	7♢
Lucky			K♢	8♢	9♡	4♠
You	6♠	6♡	A♢	3♡	4♡	6♢
Dealer			4♣	10♣	2♢	K♣

You have been high all along and have bet. You noticed that on the fourth card Dealer called, but you think he was considering raising. He may have a four flush. There is only one club exposed. Now having drawn a club for the sixth card, he is very nonchalant. Dealer drags slowly on his cigarette as the betting proceeds. He is not too interested outwardly. But wait a second. When it comes his turn, he'll grab his chips and bump it. He has probably made a flush. You had better call Clown's bet on 7s. It is bad enough that you are likely to lose on three of a kind.

Do you need a cinch to raise? Definitely not! You should raise when your chance of winning is considerably better than the average player in the pot. I know a fellow who has played poker regularly for twenty or twenty-five years. He is good at most phases of the game. He interprets the hands well. He knows the folded cards. He folds a bust. He has one fatal weakness: He doesn't raise until he is virtually a certain winner. As a result, the pots he wins tend to be smaller than the pots he loses. It never even occurs to him to raise on kings over or three 7s. "Dealer might have a straight," he reasons. When he does raise, beware. He is loaded. His opponents, who have played with him for years, all drop out if it is at all possible when he raises. They are also a little cautious about raising pots in which he plays. He doesn't seem to get wise. Instead of seizing opportunities to raise and build the pot, he seeks and usually finds reasons for not raising.

If you play poker for enjoyment, you surely want to bump it when you have a strong hand. So raise when you have the stuff. I get a big charge out of saying, "I raise."

6

I Call
Both Ways

We now turn our attention to the high-low games. My views on these games are obvious to anyone who has read the beginning pages of this book. They are more entertaining, require greater skill and provide a wider range for deceptive tactics than their ancestors. This is especially true for a Friday-night session of cards, beer and pretzels. Old Grandpappy may have bet the ranch and herd on queens full at draw against Fast Gun Willie's saloon, but, for the most part, draw and five-card stud are just a plain bore. It's more likely that Grandpa fell asleep at the table after a sizzling sequence of hands where no one had openers and dreamt it all. We'll have an adventure with an old-school player in a later chapter.

The normal transition from traditional games to high-low poker games is seven-card stud high-low. We shall study this game in detail. Let's deal with the mechanics of high-low games first.

The sequence or value of high hands is the same as in any poker game, with one addition. In wild-card games, five of a kind beats a straight flush. Low hands run as follows: the best or "perfect" low is 6, 4, 3, 2, A of assorted suits. If they are all of the same suit, it is a flush. If you declare low, it is still a flush. Similarly A, 2, 3, 4, 5 is a straight. The second best low hand is 6, 5, 3, 2, A. Then come 6, 5, 4, 2, A; 6, 5, 4, 3, A; 7, 4, 3, 2, A; and so forth. Some writers on poker treat the ace only as a high card. I have never seen it played that way. Treating the ace as either high or low adds a little jazz, which is all to the good.

In any high-low game there must be some limitation on the number of raises to each particular round of betting. Otherwise a high player with a lock and a low player with a perfect might raise indefinitely. There are two methods of limiting the raising. You either (a) limit the number of raises per person per round or (b) limit the total number of raises per round. In the first method each player is limited to one raise on each round of betting. In the second method raises are usually limited to three or four per round. The common procedure in a sociable game is a three-raise limitation. In a stiff, big-money game four raises is customary. A limitation on the total number of raises has the added feature of "killing raises." We shall see how this works later.

There is another important phase in the mechanics of high-low games. This is announcing high, low or both ways. Here also there are two methods available: (a) sequential and (b) simultaneous. In announcing sequentially the last raiser (the bettor, if there was no raising, or the high man, if everyone checked) must declare first. Then the player to his left declares and so on. In this version, there is jockeying for position on the last round of betting.

In simultaneous declaration each player takes two chips from his stack and moves both hands under the table. He returns *one* clenched fist to the center of the table. When all players are ready, the dealer announces "open." All players must open their hand immediately. The absence of a chip is a low call. The presence of one chip is a high call. Both chips present means the player is going both high and low.

It is sad but true that in most poker games the sequential

method is used. The description of simultaneous declaration may
seem forbidding. It is not. The mechanics are learned quickly.
Simultaneous declaration makes a tougher game. However, since
it is rarely played, I shall use the sequential method of announcing throughout this book.

When a player declares both ways, he must win both ways. If
he loses either way or ties for either high or low, he loses the entire pot. Consider this example in seven-card high-low.

Hog	has a flush and also a 7 low
Clown	has aces over 8s but also has an 8 low
You	have a full house
Dealer	has a 9 low and two pair

Hog	Declares both ways
Clown	Also has a two-way situation. He declares high because Hog's flush is well hidden.
You	Declare high
Dealer	Calls low. Nine low is poor; his only hope is that Hog will be beaten for high.

You split this pot with Dealer. Hog gets nothing because he is
beaten for high. Clown gets nothing because he declared high
and did not have the best high hand. The fact that his low is
better than Dealer's is ignored because Clown declared high. In
splitting the pot, it is customary for the high winner to get the
odd chip, if the pot doesn't split exactly even.

A good method if you play with an ante (no matter what
games you play) is for the dealer to ante for everyone. This
avoids all the nuisance of figuring out who "forgot" to ante. You
should try to end the game with the player to the right of the first
dealer as the last dealer. If you don't finish evenly, it is easy
enough to adjust the anteing. In a seven-man game, if five players
deal and two do not on the last round, the two players who did
not deal must square up. If the ante is 70 cents—10 cents per
man—the two non-dealers must put up fifty cents each. The five

who did deal collect 20 cents each. After this maneuver, each player has paid 50 cents for five deals.

I have never been able to understand why sandbagging is frowned on in so many circles. When you sit down to a poker game any action other than cheating should be permitted. This is especially true of a rule or method that increases the number of variables the player must learn to handle properly. Because it is a sociable game does not mean that poker must be simplified. Yet I find that check and raise is frequently not permitted and delayed raises are also not permitted. A delayed raise (or second-time-around raise) is a form of sandbagging, of course. In high-low games it is a particularly silly rule. Consider this hand:

	Down		Up		
A			K	K	Q
B			Q	J	9
You	A	4	9	6	8
C			8	5	3
D			10	10	J

A is high and bets the limit. B calls. You call. C folds. D raises. A and B call. Now it is your turn. C seemed to be a strong competitor for low at the outset. He dropped out and it now appears that you have the low uncontested. You certainly want to build this pot. If you play no sandbagging, you can't raise. You have already passed an opportunity to raise and therefore cannot raise at this point. You can only call.

Personally I prefer a wide-open game, but as sandbagging is generally not permitted in sociable games, the hands we play will outlaw sandbagging unless otherwise indicated.

End-game situations sometimes arise in high-low games where only two players remain. Unless both players immediately agree to split the pot, the hand must be played down to the end. Never concede the chance of winning both ways when there is an opportunity to do so. This is especially important if you can force your opponent to declare first.

	Down			*Up*		
You	A 3		4	5	7	7
Opponent			Q	8	4	Q

On the sixth card all other players folded. Don't agree to split this pot, as you have a lock low and your opponent is high on the board. See the last card. If it is a deuce, ace or a 7, you may have the best high hand. Even if you don't improve, make your opponent announce first. After the seventh card, if he checks, you also check. He may have a pair of queens and an 8 low and declare low, which will be an automatic win for you. In any case, he must declare first and you may want a crack at the whole pot even if he calls high.

In high-low games a three-player ending is common. When this occurs you may have a low with the others obviously struggling for high. Raise at every possible opportunity. Another typical ending is a strong low and a solid high with a "shlemiel" caught in the middle. Ordinarily this should be raised all the way. In some circles where tea is served, it is not sporting to raise in this end-game situation. If you happen to be in such a game, it is best to play with the established rules. If not—raise, raise, raise! The colloquialism covering this situation is most appropriate: the guy in the middle is "whipsawed."

As the deal proceeds, the high player on board is required to bet or check first, the same as in regular stud. Personally, I have always felt that the low man on board should be required to bet first. There is good logic to suggest this, as will be apparent in the pages which follow. Again, we shall follow the normal rules in our study.

There is an important adjustment which the beginner in high-low games must make. He is accustomed, when winning a pot, to receiving about four times the amount of money he has wagered during the entire hand. It is different in the high-low games. In an average seven- or eight-man game, there will be around four and a half or five times the amount the players that are in to the end have bet. If it is a loose game, there will be a little more. As the pot is split by the best high and the best low, you get roughly two and a half times the amount you have bet when you hold a winner. In a loose game you get a little more and in a tough game a little less. In short, in the pots you win, you get on the average of about 1½ to 1 odds. Furthermore, you must make up for the cost of the hands where you played part way, with the pots that you win. Consequently, you must win either the high side or the low in at least half of the pots where you play down to the end in high-low games, or you are playing a losing game.

The statements in the previous paragraph are general guides which you must adjust to fit the style of your game or the circumstances of each individual pot. If there are five or six players going all the way in a hand, the odds you get are better than the 1½ to 1. The 1½ to 1 assumed that about four players remain for all or most of the heavy betting. Of course, the reverse is also true. When only three players remain for the big betting, you aren't getting much in the way of odds at all. In such circumstances you must be especially careful to hold good tickets.

There is another adjustment which the beginner at high-low games must make. The size of the gamble is sharply different from comparable stakes in the standard poker games. If you are accustomed to playing draw, five-card stud and even seven-card stud at 5, 10 and 15 cents and sit down to a game at the same denominations where a variety of high-low games are played, you are in a stiffer game. The total amount of money that changes ownership at the end of an evening will be at least twice greater, or even four times as great, if you play the high-low games. It depends, of course, on which high-low games you play. A hand of draw at 5, 10 and 15 cents will cost somewhere in the range of 40 to 60 cents if played all the way. Sixty cents requires a couple of raises. Such a hand might take three minutes. A hand of twin beds at the same nominal prices will cost anywhere from a dollar to three dollars if played all the way. It will take from five to eight minutes.

These are a few of the adjustments you have to make, and it may take a few nights till you really get the feel of it. I can well remember my first evening at high-low games. I hadn't played poker for a couple of years. A next-door neighbor had a regular game that I was panting to get into. I finally made it. They were friendly and gave me fair warning. They also confined the play to a few games so it wouldn't be too confusing. What a shellacking I took! I went almost $20 into the hole in a little 5, 10 and 15 game. When it was over they complimented me on a fine performance for my first night. I thought they were kidding. A few months later when another novice arrived, I realized that they weren't kidding at all. So if you get an invitation to play in a dollar-limit high-low game with four raises per round allowed, you had better think it over carefully.

We can now go through a hand of seven-card high-low to illustrate how the game is played. Conditions are the same as in earlier chapters on the betting. Declaration of high, low or both is sequential. No sandbagging permitted. The limitation on raises is three per round of betting.

	Down		Up
A	J♡	8♣	6♣
B	3♡	7♣	A♠
C	K♣	9♢	K♠
D	5♢	9♠	J♣
E	A♡	5♡	6♡
F	J♢	10♣	Q♠
G	10♠	K♡	8♢

B is high and bets 10 cents
C calls
D drops
E calls
F calls
G calls (this is a dreadful waste of money)
A calls

Two rounds later this is the situation after a 20-cent bet had been called all around on the fourth card.

	Down		Up			
A	J♡	8♣	6♣	4♦	Q♣	A bust
B	3♡	7♣	A♠	5♣	5♠	Lots of goodies
C	K♣	9♦	K♠	4♠	9♣	Two high pair
E	A♡	5♡	6♡	7♦	Q♡	A good two-way hand
F	J♦	10♣	Q♠	A♣	4♡	Trouble
G	10♠	K♡	8♦	2♣	10♦	This pair is going to cost

B is high with fives and bets 30 cents
C raises to 60 cents
E calls
F folds
G calls
A folds
B calls (a raise would not be out of order)

The next card is dealt.

	Down		Up				
B	3♡	7♣	A♠	5♣	5♠	8♠	An 8 low
C	K♣	9♦	K♠	4♠	9♣	J♠	Two pair
E	A♡	5♡	6♡	7♦	Q♡	2♠	7 low and a four flush
G	10♠	K♡	8♦	2♣	10♦	2♡	Two pair

B bets 30 cents
C calls
E raises to 60 cents and the others call

The last card is dealt.

	Down		Up				Down	
B	3♡	7♣	A♠	5♣	5♠	8♠	2♦	7, 5 low
C	K♣	9♦	K♠	4♠	9♣	J♠	4♣	No help
E	A♡	5♡	6♡	7♦	Q♡	2♠	9♡	7, 6 low and a flush
G	10♠	K♡	8♦	2♣	10♦	2♡	Q♦	No help

B is still high and bets 30 cents. C calls. E has a two-way hand.
He decides not to raise but to wait and see what happens. He also
wants to avoid announcing first. G also calls. B is the last bettor
and therefore calls first. He declares "low." C calls high. E must
now decide whether to call high, low or both ways. Assume he
calls both ways. G calls high.

Result: B's 7, 5 low beats E's 7, 6 low. B wins low and C wins
high with kings and 9s.

That covers the mechanics of high-low games. We consider
next the problem of what to stay on for the first bet in seven-card
high-low. Remember that your play is affected by the size of the
ante and the comparative style of all other players. For this reason I am listing strong starts and optional starts separately.

There is an important feature of seven-card high-low that must
be noted, particularly by the novice. A low start sometimes converts to a high hand. A high start can hardly ever win the low
side. Every experienced player of high-low games can recall
(with much pain) the night he bet like mad on three kings
against two opposing low players, only to discover that they
weren't both low players at all. One of the opponents had bought
the "case 4" on the last card, making a small straight. The moral
is that you prefer a low start and stay only on powerful high
cards.

Strong first-round calls:

a. Any three cards 7 or lower	Excellent start, especially if includes an ace, a possible straight or two or three of same suit
b. 8 and two other low cards	Very good
c. Two cards 7 and lower and any other card	Acceptable
d. Three of a kind	Excellent
e. A pair of aces, kings, or queens and any other card	Aces and a low card is excellent

f.	Any lower pair with an ace or king kicker	A pair of 7s or lower and ace kicker is excellent
g.	Three to a flush	Very good
h.	Three in sequence	Very good

Optional first-round calls:

Stay for the first bet with the following hands if it is a sociable low-stakes game, the ante is large, the play is loose, or you are riding a winning streak. Be wary of your subsequent action if there is no marked improvement on the fourth card.

i.	Ace, 8 and a high card	Eight is a troublesome low
j.	8, a low card and any other card with added feature	Third card must make a pair, a two flush, a two straight, or be a king. Fold if next card doesn't improve the hand.
k.	Any pair	Fold if no improvement on next card
l.	Any two flush with an added feature	Must include an ace or king or two straight. Fold early if no improvement.
m.	A broken straight with only one hole in it	8, 9, J, but not 8, 10, Q. Must improve this quickly.

We can now study subsequent action with an illustrative hand.

	Down		*Up*	
A			Q♦	Out
B			A♡	10♣
C			K♠	A♠
You	8♠	Q♠	2♡	
D			J♣	Out
E			8♡	9♠
F			3♦	8♦

You stayed with this holding only because it is a sociable, loose game. It is about as poor a start as you ever want to stay on. An 8 low is no great shakes, unless there is no apparent strength on the low side. Assume that A and D dropped on the first bet. Consider each of the following as your fourth card. C has bet 20 cents in the usual 10, 20 and 30 game.

1. 6◇   Call; there is no apparent strength for low

2. 7♡   Call, but this is marginal. There is a remarkable difference between an 8, 7 low and an 8, 6 low. Change F to a 3, 2 and you can fold.

3. J♠   Call; flush possibilities have been weakened by the appearance of two more spades. There are now seven spades remaining in the deck.

4. 2♣   Fold; there may be some strong high hands to contend with in this layout

5. Q♣   Call; nothing here to be excited with

Assume that you drew the 6◇ and called. E drops and all others call. Study the next layout. The folded cards are Q◇, J♣, 8♡, 9♠.

	Down		Up		
B			A♡	10♣	10◇
C			K♠	A♠	9♡
You	Q♠	8♠	2♡	6◇	
F			3◇	8◇	3♠

B bets 30 cents, C calls, and your fifth card is:

1. A♣   Call or raise, with the raise highly recommended. You raise for two reasons: (1) You want this pot to be big, as it looks as though you have a good prospect of winning. (2) You must build the image of a very strong low player. If F develops a two-way hand, you want

him to be afraid to contest your powerful-looking low.

2. 7♣   Same situation as in 1. on the surface—call or raise. You may develop a very weak 8, in which case the need for deception is great.

3. 6♣   Optional—leaning toward a call; you may still bring in the low, but the betting is getting steep. If you stay, it is because the competition for low seems limited.

4. 8♣   Fold or raise to create a deceptive image of a good low.

5. Q♣   Optional to call or fold. You have invested only 40 cents. The big bets are coming and this hand is marginal. If you fold, don't be upset if someone steals the low with a 9 or nothing. All the hands would have ended differently and you'll never know what might have happened. Take the small loss and relax. If you stay and don't improve on the next card, get out.

Suppose that you actually got the 7♣. You bumped it to 60 cents. All the players called and the next card was dealt.

	Down		Up			
B			A♡	10♣	10◇	Q♡
C			K♠	A♠	9♡	9♣
You	Q♠	8♠	2♡	6◇	7♣	
F			3◇	8◇	3♠	5◇

B checks. C bets 30 cents. Consider your sixth card as:

1. A♣   Raise; F can have an 8 low, which probably beats your 8, or a flush or both. He may have three of a kind.

2. J♠   Raise or fold. You should act the role of a solid low player if you choose to play.

Assume you get the A♣ and raise to 60 cents. F raises to 90 cents. B, who apparently started with two low hole cards, folds. An expert high-low player in the C seat would raise no matter what his closed cards are. His reasoning would be the reverse of yours. He must attempt to force F into a low call if F ends up with both a high and low. Equally important, he accomplishes this at no significant cost, as you will certainly raise to $1.20 on 7, 6, 2, A. His alternative is to kill the last (third) raise by raising a dime, but in this situation it would be an incredible action to show such weakness. Assume he raises to $1.20 and this bet is called.

You are dealt an indifferent high card in the hole for your final card. A 3 or 4 would have wrapped it up pretty good, but you

have drawn very well in the middle rounds of this hand and can't
complain. You have an 8, 7 low. C bets; you raise. F calls, waiting
for some useful information. C raises to 90 cents and you raise to
$1.20. You call low. C will obviously call high when it is his turn.
F does have an 8, 5 low and a diamond flush with 2◊, K◊, 4♡ in
the hole and 3◊, 3♠, 5◊, 8◊ up.

He can call high on the flush, low on the 8, 5, or both ways.
No kings were revealed and he saw only one other 9, which
makes C a great big question mark. He is also facing 7, 6, 2, A
in your hand and can easily be beaten for low. How anyone can
prefer five-card stud to this sizzler is a mystery, provided it is
action you want!

7

Friday Night
at Freddie's House

Freddie was bubbling over as the gang assembled. He had settled an accident claim for a client earlier that morning. After a
hard two-hour session with the insurance-company adjuster, a
settlement of $3,800 was arranged. The previous day in consulta-
tion with his client they had agreed to accept $1,000, but Freddie
wheedled a much larger settlement. He spoke softly at times,
harshly at other times. He asked for $5,000. The adjuster finally
offered $2,000. Freddie stared at the ceiling to cover the warm
glow spreading inside. They bargained some more and finally
settled. (Freddie might have made good at table stakes.) With
almost $1,300 as his share, Freddie met his client for lunch. Over
steaming shishkebab and wine, the papers were signed. Freddie
returned to the insurance-company office for the check. He
phoned Eleanor, who arranged for a sitter. She called Al at his
office to tell him the good news and to get the name of his tailor.
Fred met Eleanor at 3:30 at a cocktail lounge downtown. They
wafted a couple of martinis, caught a taxi over to the tailor's,
where Fred ordered a custom-fitted, three-button drape model
for 175 (when you buy in this bracket, the dollar sign isn't
shown). Alice ordered some drapery material she had been ey-

ing for months. On the way home, they stopped at Henri's for
Chateaubriand for two with an imported wine, and topped it
with a couple of brandy liqueurs. They arrived home at ten of
nine, just in time to pay the baby sitter and get the den set for
the poker game. It was the beginning of an exciting weekend as
Eleanor headed for the phone to set up a party for Saturday
night.

Although the day had been invigorating and pleasant, the
poker session was a disaster. Freddie played on everything and
paid little attention to the game. He was in a daze most of the

time. Just as he imagined himself arguing an important issue of
constitutional law before the Supreme Court, this little number
came up:

		Down		Up	
Fred	J♣	6♡	8♠		
Bill			K♠		
Paul			A♢		
Herb			7♣		
Jim			5♢		
Al			7♠		
Frank			9♢		

Paul bet 10 cents. Frank folded but all others called. Freddie
could have folded with this hodgepodge, but there was no stopping him tonight and this start wasn't too bad.

Two rounds later, after a 20-cent bet called all around, this was
the layout:

		Down		Up	
Fred	J♣	6♡	8♠	J♡	4♣
Bill			K♠	9♣	K♢
Paul			A♢	5♡	J♠
Herb			7♣	10♢	10♡
Jim			5♢	6♣	Q♣
Al			7♠	J♢	5♠

Bill bet 30 cents
Paul called
Herb dropped
Jim called
Al raised to 60 cents
Fred called
Bill raised to 90 cents
Paul raised 10 cents to $1, killing the raises
All others called

Fred's play is pure charity. His jacks are now dead. His best prospect is an 8, 6 low, and he needs two excellent draws to make that. If he's lucky enough to get two good low cards, he may not win, as there seem to be some strong lows working; but Fred stayed for $1.

He next drew the 5♣. Observing that he had the chance of making a straight as well as an 8, 6 low on J♣, 6♡, 8♠, J♡, 4♣, 5♣, Freddie was hooked for another dollar. He could have held the bet to 80 cents by raising a dime when it came his turn, but he didn't. Freddie rarely kills a raise for a dime, as he won't permit himself to show weakness. By playing this way he also permits himself to lose more than he might.

On the final card Freddie drew a small pair. His holding was now two pair for high and a jack low. There were four players in the game; Paul had dropped on the sixth card. Bill bet 30 and Herb called. Al raised to 60. At this point Fred decided to play cagey. He had observed Al making odd-looking plays. Freddie raised to 90 cents. Bill hesitated, a little confused by Fred's sudden show of strength. He thought a bit and then raised to $1.20. This final (third) raise was called all around. Bill, the last raiser, called high. The other calls were low, low and high. Bill won high with kings over. Al had 7, 5 low, which beat Jim's 7, 6.

This hand is typical of Fred's play in seven-card high-low. He shifts about from one prospective hand to another, when none is a very solid possibility. When in doubt he stays, and Freddie is frequently in doubt. Hooked for a small amount at the outset, he gets in deeper and deeper as the betting mounts. This pot cost him $3.60.

But nothing could stop Fred after his big deal earlier in the day. This was the next hand after the fifth card. There had been no raising on the first two rounds of betting.

	Down		*Up*		
Frank			Q♠	K♡	3♣
Fred	A♣	3◊	7◊	2◊	6♣
Paul			7♡	Q♡	4◊
Al			K◊	A♡	K♣

Al bet 30 cents
Frank called
Fred raised
Paul called
Al raised to 90 cents
Frank dropped
Fred raised to $1.20
All called

The sixth card was dealt.

	Down		*Up*			
Fred	A♣	3◊	7◊	2◊	6♣	Q◊
Paul			7♡	Q♡	4◊	3♠
Al			K◊	A♡	K♣	6♡

Al bet 30. Fred raised to 60. Paul called. Al raised to 90. Fred bumped it to $1.20. All called.

Fred's seventh card was the 9 of diamonds. He now had a flush and a 7, 6 low. Fred had consumed two cans of beer, on top of wine at lunch and dinner, plus a couple of martinis earlier in the day. He made no effort to conceal his excitement. Al bet 30 cents. Fred, who had his chips all ready, blurted 60.

Paul, a strong, seasoned veteran in the high-low department, shuddered; he held a 7, 5 low. He sensed that Al was setting Freddie up. He considered raising to try to shift the first call away from Freddie, but finally concluded that it would not change his own situation, and in any case Al could avoid the first call if he chose to. Paul called.

Al merely called. Freddie, with 60 cents ready for another raise, was surprised. With no further thought or concern, he announced both ways. Paul went into a huddle. He was now even more convinced that Al had Fred beat one way or the other. He finally declared low. As he turned a 2, 3, 5 in the hole, Al said, "I'm low and it takes a perfect to beat me."

He raked in all the chips, as there was no high winner.

Al's low hand was well hidden, but an important sign Freddie should not have missed was that Paul never "killed a raise." Facing Fred's strong 7, 6 low on top, Paul never raised a dime but permitted both the fifth- and sixth-card rounds to reach $1.20. More critical was Fred's action on the last round. He should not have raised if he was considering going for the whole pot. He should have called the last round and forced Al to declare first. Fred actually held the poorest low of the three.

On the next hand Fred stayed on K, J, 8 of assorted suits. He picked up a 10 as his next card and called for 20 cents. On the fifth card he made a pair of 8s. This pulled him in for the next round at a cost of 60 cents. He received a seven-spot. Needing a 9 for a straight, Freddie noted that two 9s were on board. He did not recall that Paul had folded a 9 on the first card. He now had one draw for the case 9 out of 31 unexposed cards. He didn't pull it, but Freddie did get another 10 for two pair. He was now sucked into the final round at a cost of 80 cents and lost to an apparent low player who had aces over 6s well hidden.

A half hour later Fred retired to the bathroom to soak his face in cold water. He sipped some hot coffee and returned to the fray. On the next hand he pulled a 7 low to win half of a large pot. Then Freddie pulled this little baby: A♡, 3♡ in the hole and 2♠ up. Another good pot would bring him up to only a four or five bucks' loser, he mused. (It really would have been closer to ten.) His next card was the J♠. He was still strong. Next he pulled the 9♡. For his sixth card he drew the 3◇. Fred's hand was now A♡, 3♡, 2♠, J♠, 9♡, 3◇. The prospects were dim, as a strong low and a powerful high were both raising. The 3s were dead and an ace was exposed. His only reasonable hope was to pull an ace. Fortunately for Fred he didn't and was spared calling the final bet, as the high was won on three 10s. As he didn't get a winner's share and instead dropped about $2.50, Fred was now losing almost $20. With another hour or so of play remaining, Fred managed to win another half of a small pot and finished the night $29 behind. "Lost a little over twenty," he announced.

Several years ago I was invited by a friend to substitute in a game. I played with them about a half dozen times in the course of a year or more when one of the regulars couldn't make it. It was an average game as to quality, played for small stakes. When the crowd assembled, a sandwich spread, a case of beer and a large pot of coffee were already available. This was not too unusual. What was different about these fellows was that they really socked it away. Practically all the players present polished off two or three combination sandwiches, a couple of beers, and lots of coffee. The edges of the table were littered with coffee cups, crusts of bread, and so forth. They kidded around all through the evening, and I finally asked whether all this food was in place of dinner. They only stared at me.

When the game ended I totaled up my chips and was waiting to be paid off. One of the players yanked an oversized, frayed, ancient sheet of paper from his back pocket and unfolded it. As each player cashed in his chips, he reported his result for the evening. It was duly recorded. If there was an imbalance after everyone had reported, a complete review was required. No fancy rounding was permitted. After the results for that evening were properly recorded, a cumulative total was made for each player and publicly announced.

The subdivision of homes in their area had been built six years earlier. This crowd had been playing on Friday nights all of the six years, and the large tattered sheet was six years old. No illusions were permitted here, as every player's score for the entire period was on public display. It seemed a little sadistic. If the Freddie of this game (there is always a Freddie) wanted to round his result a little, why not let him?

8

MAC: Act I
The Man with the Cigar

It was a long holiday weekend. Al's sister-in-law came to visit with her family. Al had met Mac, his brother-in-law, a number of times in the past but only for short periods. He knew Mac as an ambitious, aggressive and sometimes overbearing salesman type. Mac had recently been promoted to the job of sales manager of his firm. This was an achievement of which Mac was justly proud. It also added a bit to his desire always to be right.

On the first day of the weekend Al discovered that Mac was a poker player. "Yeah, I just love a good game of five-card stud at table stakes," Mac said as he gently tapped his cigar on the ash tray. Al explained that he also played poker but that he preferred high-low games. Mac roared with laughter at the notion that anyone would even compare these wild games with five-card stud. "Why, five-card stud is all skill. You know what you have and you can really play those cards. I just read *Poker According to Maverick* and he said of high-low seven-card stud that skill is almost no factor and all you need is dumb luck to win." Mac was quoting correctly. Al had also read the Maverick book and recalled the statement.*

"Of course, those crazy games may be good for a laugh—imagine losing on four of a kind—but they are not real poker," Mac continued. Al changed the subject. He had run into these hardheads before and knew that there was no point in arguing. Years ago he would have started explaining that there were more variables to handle and so forth. He gave it up in favor of changing the subject to baseball, politics, sex, or what have you.

Marie had invited some couples over that evening to meet her sister, Ellen, and brother-in-law. Al didn't know how it started, but at one point he returned from the kitchen with some liquid and found the company getting set to play poker. Some of the women were nuts about the high-low games and never missed a chance to play. The stakes were 2 cents and 4 cents. Mac played, of course, and he won $1.60. He enjoyed every minute of it.

The next day Mac was hinting around for some real action. Al ignored it. Finally at lunch Mac said point-blank that he enjoyed the games the previous evening and wanted to play again for real stakes. It wasn't poker, but it was entertaining. Al obliged. Frank, Bill and Paul were available. They were in the 10, 20,

* *Poker According to Maverick*, Dell Publishing Co., Inc., 1959, p. 113.

30 regular Friday-night game but didn't mind stronger medicine. Walt and Jerry would come. Both were big-money players.

The conditions were set:

Stakes were 25, 50 and $1
Sandbagging in any form permitted
Ante 25 cents—25 cents on first bet and any amount on later bets
Sequential declaration
Four raises per round

Mac puffed at his cigar as a hand of seven-card high-low was dealt.

	Down		Up
Frank			8♡
Walt			4♡
Al			7♠
Mac	10♣	Q♡	K♠
Jerry			9♣
Bill			3♡
Paul			3♣

Al would have folded Mac's hand immediately. In a smaller game he might play with this holding. Mac had no idea what a stiff game this was. He was accustomed to playing table stakes and this seemed like a small game to him. He also hadn't learned much the night before. It all seemed like luck, just as Maverick had predicted, and he had been lucky.

Mac bet a quarter. Jerry and Frank folded. The others called. Mac drew a 10 for his next card. He was still high and bet a dollar. The others called and Paul dealt another card.

	Down		*Up*		
Walt			4♡	K♡	A♣
Al			7♠	2♠	9♢
Mac	10♣	Q♡	K♠	10♢	8♠
Bill			3♡	8♢	6♡
Paul			3♣	5♢	4♢

Walt bet $1
Al called
Mac raised to $2
Bill called
Paul raised to $3
All called

The next card was dealt.

	Down		*Up*			
Walt			4♡	K♡	A♣	9♠
Al			7♠	2♠	9♢	Q♢
Mac	10♣	Q♡	K♠	10♢	8♠	8♣
Bill			3♡	8♢	6♡	6♠
Paul			3♣	5♢	4♢	J♠

Mac bet $1 on 10s and 8s
Bill called
Paul raised to $2
Walt folded
Al folded
Mac, now satisfied that he was bucking two low players,
   raised to $3
Bill called
Paul raised to $4
Mac raised to $5 (the fourth raise)

Mac pulled the ace of spades, surveyed the table and bet $1.
Bill raised to $1.25. Paul just called. Mac was confused by the
weakness (he thought) shown by both players. He tried to

conceal it with a brash announcement, $2.25. Bill studied the cards, then raised to $3.25. Paul called. Mac mumbled something about Bill's sandbag. He considered raising, when it dawned on him that all this funny stuff had something to do with the order of announcing high or low. He just called, and this permitted him to declare third.

Bill, the last raiser, called high. Paul called low. Mac called high. Paul folded his cards and reached for the pot. Bill showed 6s full. Turning to Paul, Bill said, "Dammit, you stole the low with a small straight."

Paul grinned. "You'll never know."

Mac assumed an air of confidence and smiled knowingly as he tried to regain his composure. His $25 stack of chips was more than half gone. He turned the next hand with a knowledgeable flip. "Queen down." On the following hand Mac was dealt A♠, 6♠, 10♡. He stayed for a quarter and drew 10♠. He bet a dollar. Two players called, and Al, who was to Mac's right, raised to $2. Mac raised to $3. The other two players folded. Mac reached for the center of the table: "Split it."

"No, let's play. Raise to $4," said Al.

Mac knew that Al had every right to require that the hand be played to the end. It had happened once the previous night in the penny game. He called and the next card was dealt.

	Down			Up	
Al			3◇	7♣	Q◇
Mac	A♠	6♠	10♡	10♠	8♠

Mac began to like this hand, as he had a four flush, a high pair and the makings of an eight low. He decided on a display of strength and the betting reached $5. Mac bought another stack of chips. He was unaware of the danger of being high on board in a two-man ending. The war of nerves continued after the next card.

	Down		Up			
Al			3◊	7♣	Q◊	8◊
Mac	A♠	6♠	10♡	10♠	8♠	9♣

Mac noted the three diamonds in Al's hand but decided he could not afford to show weakness. The bet again reached $5. As the next card was dealt, Mac plotted. He would bet out strongly and fondle his chips as though prepared to raise. When Al raised, he would just call. But Al didn't raise, and Mac had to announce first. His final card was the 4♣. He now had a 9 low and 10s for high.

He studied the 3◊, 7♣, Q◊, 8◊. Al could hold anything from four of a kind to a 7 low. He began to wonder why Al had insisted on playing it out, speculating about a diamond flush. He came to a decision: "Low."

"Low," Al said, turning the 2♣, 5♡, K♠. "My 8 low is a lock."

Mac should never have raised with these cards. He should have checked each round and held the bet to a maximum of $1.

Mac was now stuck for over $30. Satisfied that it was bad luck which would change shortly, he plunged ahead. He won a pot on a 6 low. Then he lost a tough one with a straight. Mac insisted on playing high hands, even though he noted that the others shied away from staying in on high cards at the start. He stayed on 4, 4, Q, drew a jack and called. He drew a 10 and stayed for $3.50. He pulled another jack and stayed for $4.25. He didn't improve on the final card. The final bet was again $4.25, and Mac didn't even kill a raise when he had a chance at it. He lost to three 7s.

When it was Mac's turn he dealt five-card stud. He found that the boys knew that game pretty well, as each hand was played rapidly and skillfully. His deal lasted two or three minutes. The high-low games took from five to eight minutes each. Then Mac announced "Draw and guts to open" and with a flourish he passed the cards to be cut. "This will sure be a rough one," Jerry said with a twinkle as he cut them.

When they broke for a snack at 11:30, Mac was down $70

and he was mumbling about slow playing and wasting time for a sandwich and beer. As Marie brought the refreshments into the den she asked Mac if he was enjoying himself. Mac braced himself: "Fine. Just fine."

End of Act I.

9

Decisions, Decisions, Decisions

Fred had missed the 6:02 commuter special from the city. When he boarded the 6:25 he had spotted Al settling down in a seat at the rear of the smoking car. Fred joined Al and they had a pleasant chat. Eventually the conversation drifted onto poker.

FRED: I just don't care for three-card substitution. It's too slow. If you drop out of a hand, you have to wait as much as ten minutes.

AL: Come on, Fred. You know that three-card sub is the best game we play. It calls for more difficult decisions than any of our other games. You have to keep your mind on the game and know what is going on all the time. If you would pay a little more attention to the other players and to their cards, you would enjoy the game better.

FRED: It's too damned expensive anyway.

AL: Why don't you suggest reducing the stakes? There is no point in sacrificing the best game because it is a little steeper than the others.

FRED: Well, I don't like it. The dealer has an advantage in three-card substitution.

AL: The dealer does have an advantage, but we rectify that by playing only in complete cycles so that each player deals it an equal number of times during the evening.

FRED: But then I have to deal a game I don't like just so I am not placed at a disadvantage.

AL: Think about this for a second. Think about the guys in the game who seem to like three-card sub and those who don't like it. You thinking?

FRED: Just a second.

AL: No offense intended, Fred, but don't you conclude that the stronger players like three-card substitution and others do not like it?

FRED: I know that I'm no giant at poker. I play for the fun of it and if I lose a few bucks I don't mind. An evening in the city costs twenty or twenty-five dollars, and I enjoy poker more than having dinner at a crowded, noisy restaurant and sitting through a lousy play or movie. I even enjoy the penny game with the women.

AL: A couple of the girls have gotten to be pretty good players. It's sure different from two years ago when they each needed a list at their elbow to show the sequence of hands. When we started, Carol didn't know whether a full house beat a flush, and last week she was panting for her deal to start a round of three-card substitution.

The train rolled to a halt, and Fred and Al rose to depart. Al suggested lunch the next day. "Can't," said Fred. "I'm tied up with a client on a rough tax problem. If I can work this out for him, I might get all of his business. That would really put me over. See you Friday."

Three-card substitution is a high-low game. It proceeds like five-card stud, but after the betting on the fifth card each player in sequence is permitted to discard and draw a card. He may discard an up card or his hole card. After the first substitution there is a round of betting. There is next another substitution and a round of betting, followed by a third substitution and the final round of betting. A player may reject the opportunity to substitute (or draw). The substitutions are not free. In a 10, 20, 30 game, the first draw costs 30 cents. The second costs 60 cents and the final trade costs 90 cents. In a 2- and 4-cent game, the substitutions cost 4, 8 and 12 cents.

First-round calls:

  a. Any two cards 7 or lower
  b. Any pair; but beware of two small pair in the end game
  c. 8 and a lower card; be careful—an 8 low can be very expensive in this game
  d. Two of the same suit when an ace is included; but fold A♡, 10♡ if the next card is not a heart, a pair, or an 8 or lower
  e. Ace, king or ace, queen; this must be improved on the next card

Optional first-round calls:

    f. Two of the same suit ⎫ Fold any of these if the next
    g. 7 or lower and a high card ⎬ card doesn't help in some man-
    h. Two in sequence ⎭ ner

Never call the first bet on two high cards unmatched in any
way. Fold an 8 and a high card. An ace is a powerful card in
this game, and a hidden pair of aces sometimes creates a very
deceptive situation. In a seven- or eight-man game, most of the
cards are used if four or five players stay to the end. Consequently, it is most important to be alert and remember the cards
that have been turned. It is not an uncommon problem, for
example, to be holding 2♡, 3♣, 4♡, 7♡, J♡ in your first five
cards. You are now faced with a critical problem of whether
to discard the jack and try for low or to discard the 3 and try
for a heart flush. No such problem arises in seven-card high-low.
You raise and sit back smugly waiting for the flush, the low or
both to come in. If you make neither, you may also win half the
pot because of the situation you created by raising.

In making the decision of whether to go for the flush or low,
you must weigh all the available evidence. Had you seen no
cards other than your own, you would know that a 7 low can be
made with any one of twelve remaining cards—four aces, four
5s and four 6s. There are only nine more hearts, so the low
would be the better gamble. But, of course, you do see the table
and you have noted the cards that were folded—at least those
that concern you. Only three hearts have been exposed and you
have seen three aces, two 5s and one 6. That means there are
six low cards and six hearts—a toss-up.

But that doesn't end the problem. Will a flush win? Will any
7 low win? What about an 8 low? Study the table again. Another player looks as though he is going flushing, and if he hits
it, he'll have an ace-high flush. On the other hand, 7, 6 might
not make it, as one of the guys has bet strongly on what looks like

a 7, 5 possibility. And so it goes—for this problem and for a number of others that come up in this game.

Generally it takes a good hand to win. Consequently you don't go for 8 low or expect 9s and 7s to win high unless the board suggests little competition in that direction. An important point of decision is after the fifth card is dealt. The earlier betting is ordinarily mild. From this point on, it will cost plenty. If you hold A♠, 7♡, J♢, 4♠, Q♣ after the fifth card, you need two good draws to make a low. Furthermore, you may make the 7 low and lose, which is sad indeed. There is little in the world as pitiful as the guy who drew the card he wanted and lost anyway.

Not long ago I held two pair, 10s and 6s after the fifth card. I dropped! The competition for high looked tough. The 10s and 6s were dead. My investment was small and it was the best action. The high side was won by a player trying to improve a pair of kings, which he never did. Another prospective high failed to make a straight on three tries. A hand that looked like a flush went low instead, as the low competition was light. The low winner made it by breaking a pair. As my cards were dead, I would not have traded, so all the draws would have been the same if I had stayed. I would have won the high. My two pair had been on the table for all the world to see. My reputation had been damaged, but I'm sure that my pocketbook had not. If the same exact situation were repeated thousands of times with all the unseen cards considered in all possible combinations, I am satisfied that my action would prove to be the winning one. In short, I made the correct percentage play and happened to get hit with one of the instances when the result went against the odds. Long shots do come in occasionally.

Let's go through a sample hand, starting from the fifth card:

	Down		*Up*			
A	10◊	8♠	Out			Correct to fold
B	J◊	J♠	9◊	5♡	5♠	Two pair can be a problem
C	4♡	3♡	8◊	K◊	8♡	An 8 low went sour
D	A♣	Q♠	A♠	K♡	10♠	Looks like a pinochle hand
E	7♠	5◊	9♠	6♠	4♠	Can end up either way
F	4◊	8♣	6◊	2◊	J♣	An 8, 6 prospect with three diamonds
G	6♣	10♣	10♡	7♡	Q◊	Weak

G checks

B bets 30 cents

C calls

D calls

E raises to 60 cents

G folds, but all others call

The first substitution began. The underlined card indicates the discard. Note that each player sees the card obtained by the player to his right before he decides on his discard. This gives the dealer a significant advantage. To equalize the dealer's advantage it is necessary to deal a whole round of three-card substitution.

	Down		*Up*			*Draw*
B	J◊	J♠	9◊	5♡	5♠	Q♣
C	4♡	3♡	8̲◊	K◊	8♡	7♣
D	A♣	Q♠	A♠	K̲♡	10♠	K♣
E	7♠	5◊	9♠	6♠	4̲♠	A◊
F	4◊	8♣	6̲◊	2◊	J̲♣	3♣

B has no problem; he tries for the full house. One J and one

5 are still live. His chance of improving is not good, but he can't sit with this. Besides, this draw costs only 30 cents.

C pitches the king in a combination play for a low or a heart.

When he throws the 10, it is clear that D has a big pair. He hits.

E gives up the chance for a flush. By throwing the 9♠ he gets a crack at both a low or straight. His buy is excellent.

Seeing the good draw by E, F is not too pleased, but he also draws well

D bets 30 on kings
E raises to 60
F makes it 70
B raises to 80, which kills the raises
C folds and others call

On the next round B and D trade but fail to improve. E stands pat. F has a problem but also doesn't draw. It is pretty tough to break an 8, 6.

The next round of betting is exactly as before—30, 60, 70, 80. On the final trade B fails to make the full house. D also draws because B might have three 5s. E and F stand pat. B stays for 80 cents on the final bet to "keep him honest." F also calls.

D and E split the pot. E concludes the hand with a 7, 6, and D takes the high on aces over kings.

Assume you have stayed with 6♡, 3♣, drew the J♣ on the third card and now the fourth card is dealt. The ante, stakes and conditions are the usual. What is your action in each of the six problems noted, after C bets 30 cents on the pair of kings?

	Down	*Up*		
A		10◇	Out	
B		2♡	8◇	Q◇
C		K♣	5◇	K♡
You	3♣	6♡	J♣	
D		7♠	A♡	Q♠
E		10♠	8♣	2♠
F		9♠	Out	

1. A♣   4. 8♠
2. 9◇   5. J◇
3. 5♡   6. 9♣

Comments:

1. Call; prospects for low are good and you have three clubs
2. Fold
3. Call
4. Call; not nearly so good as 3
5. Fold
6. Call

Assume you pulled the 8♠ and called. All the others called and the next card was dealt.

	Down	*Up*			
B		2♡	8◇	Q◇	5♡
C		K♣	5◇	K♡	2♣
You	3♣	6♡	J♣	8♠	
D		7♠	A♡	Q♠	3◇
E		10♠	8♣	2♠	3♡

C is still high with kings, and bets 30 cents. What is your action with each of the following cards?

1. J◇   3. 7♡
2. 5♠   4. 10♣

Comments:

1. Fold even though no jacks are exposed. C will be a tough hand to compete against and it may be costly. Kings are also very live.
2. Call
3. Fold; the low competition is apt to be most severe, and an 8, 7 low isn't likely to win it. D may start raising and it will become quite costly.
4. Fold. What else?

Assume that you pulled the 5♠ and called. D raised to 60; E went out; B raised to 70; C made it $1 and you and the others called.

The trading went as indicated below:

	Down	Up				Draw
B		2♡	8◇	Q◇	5♡	5♣
C		K♣	5◇	K̄♡	2♣	A◇
You	3♣	6♡	J̄♣	8♠	5♠	A♣
D	7♠	7♠	Ā♡	Q♠̲	3◇	K◇

C bets 30 cents and it is your turn. You have drawn well, while both B and D have drawn poorly on the first substitutions. There are now two strategies open to you.

a. You can call the 30 cents, in which case both B and D will probably call. You can then refuse the next two trades and wait to see what happens to B and D. They may both out-draw you. If neither of them improves with the second and third trades, you can raise on the last bet and they may have to call. You will have passed up two rounds of raises.
b. You can raise in the hopes that they will not outdraw you and that the pot will be built up. A raise is not likely to drive either B or D out unless they are weak in their down card and aren't much competition anyway. There is also

an outside chance that B is a high player. If you raise, both B and D may raise a dime. If they do not raise the dime, they will surely have powerful low prospects, and C will reraise. Following up your strategy, you would then make it $1.20.

The choice is whether to play primarily to limit your possible loss or to go for a big pot by raising. The correct action in this situation is to limit your possible loss. The competition for low is too severe on an 8, 6 which all can see. You probably have two competitors for low, and C has no competitors for high. Your best choice in this situation is to play it tight.

10

MAC: Act II
Disaster

The boys had all eaten and returned to the den. It was around midnight as they started a round of three-card substitution. Mac had liked the game the night before when they played for pennies. Al had warned him to play cautiously in this game. The substitutions were $1, $2 and $3, and with four raises per round a single pot could cost over twenty bucks. Mac had inspected his cigar as he announced that he could take care of himself.

In the first pot, Mac stayed for a quarter on 2♠, 10♡. This was no tragedy in a penny game, but it was a boner in this game. He drew an 8♡ and stayed for a 50-cent bet. His fourth card was a 7♣. He stayed for $2. At this point there were three players in the game, and this was the layout after the next card was dealt:

	Down		Up		
Al		3♣	Q♠	9♡	Q◇
Mac	2♠	10♡	8♡	7♣	A♠
Bill		2♣	4♡	J◇	6♡

Al bet $1. Mac called. Bill raised to $2. Al raised to $3. The others called. They made the first substitution for $1.

	Down		Up			Draw
Al		3♣	Q♠	9♡	Q◇	
Mac	2♠	10♡	8♡	7♣	A♠	5♡
Bill		2♣	4♡	J◇	6♡	7◇

Al played it pat. Mac pitched the 10 and picked up a 5 for an 8, 7 low. Bill pitched the jack and picked up a 7. Mac stared at Bill's cards. Al bet $1. Mac assumed Bill had a strong low and raised to $1.25, to kill a raise, but Bill only called. Al raised to $2.25. Mac stared harder and wondered whether Bill had paired the 7. Finally Mac raised to $3.25. Bill called. Al raised to $4.25.

Al didn't draw. "Play these," Mac announced as he dragged on his stogie. Mac was surprised when Bill also refused the draw. Al bet $1. Mac studied the hands, which were:

	Down		Up		
Al		3♣	Q♠	9♡	Q◇
Mac	2♠	5♡	8♡	7♣	A♠
Bill		2♣	4♡	7◇	6♡

Mac concluded that Bill had an 8 in the hole and that Bill was hoping that Mac had a 6. In that case, 8, 7, 6, 4 would beat 8, 7, 6, 5. But he actually had a deuce and his 8, 7, 5, 2 would beat

Bill. This would be an amusing hand to tell his cronies about. Mac raised to $2. Bill called and the bet rapidly reached $5.

They all stood pat for the last trade. The bet again reached $5. Bill didn't have an 8 in the hole. He had a 5. Mac was silent as he pondered this one. The bastard wanted to be sure I didn't draw and acted weak. I raised for him too! I'll remember that little gadget.

The pot cost Mac $20.25.

Mac was next dealt a 9♠ down and a 10♡ up. Having read Maverick rather than the previous chapter, he liked the hand. His next card was the 7♡. The bet was only a half, so he stayed and pulled a pair of 9s. Four players called a dollar bet, and after the next card the table looked like this:

	Down	*Up*			
Frank		A♠	6♠	Q♣	4◇
Walt		4♡	J♣	6◇	A♡
Al		2◇	6♡	10♠	K♣
Mac	9♠	10♡	7♡	9♣	8◇

Frank was high and bet $1. When it came Mac's turn, he bumped to $2. All called.

Frank paid $1, pitched the Q♣ and pulled the 8♠. Walt tossed the J♣ and pulled the 3◊. Al ditched the 10♠ and pulled a 2♠.

Mac pondered Al's play. The folded cards, he recalled, included a jack but no kings. There were one 6 and two jacks remaining in about thirty cards. He would have three cracks at it, which gave him a fair gamble to make the straight. Mac was also convinced that Al had a king in the hole for kings over deuces. So he paid his dollar and drew a hole card.

It was the 9♡! Had he played the pair he would have made three 9s.

Al checked his deuces! When he realized it was his turn, Mac also checked. Frank checked. Walt bet a dollar and all called.

	Down	Up			
Frank		A♠	6♠	8♠	4◊
Walt		4♡	3◊	6◊	A♡
Al		2◊	6♡	2♠	K♣
Mac	9♡	10♡	7♡	9♣	8◊

Frank and Walt stood pat. Al pitched his hole card for $2! Al's play now became clear, for Mac learns fast and is ordinarily quite handy at the card table. Al's original hole card was a little one. He tossed the 10 first because the king was live, but he had really been playing low. In fact, he would have gone out if the next card hadn't helped. As the king was very live, he held it in preference to the 10. When he pulled the pair of deuces Al decided to stay because the bet was only $1 and he (Mac) had pulled a hole card and checked so that the high competition seemed limited.

Three 9s would have been solid for high! Mac concluded that he would now go for two pair in an effort to salvage the situation. This analysis was sound, but he didn't make another pair on two successive tries for $2 and $3, and Al did pull a second pair.

Mac stayed out of the next one with 9♣, Q♡. He also folded

6♡, Q♠! He was learning. On the fifth hand of three-card substitution, Mac started with 5♡, A♡. He bet and pulled the 7♣.
He was high again and bet $1. His next card was the A♠. After
a $1 bet he pulled the 3♡. Here was the layout at this point:

	Down		*Up*		
Mac	5♡	A♡	7♣	A♠	3♡
Jerry		4♣	7♡	Q◇	3◇
Paul		9♠	4♠	4◇	J♠
Frank		A♣	6♣	2♠	10♣

This was going to be a difficult decision for Mac. He would,
of course, have been in a far more comfortable situation if he
were in last position and could see the actions taken by the
others. Perhaps the betting would be informative. He bet $1
and the others merely called. After a long huddle, Mac decided
to stay with the aces. A 7 was showing and another had been
folded earlier, so he pitched his 7 of clubs. This also permitted
him to hold three hearts. He drew the K♠. Jerry dropped the
queen and pulled a 9. Paul pitched the 9 and also received a
king. Frank discarded the 2♠ and drew a club, which gave him
four clubs on the board. Mac was discouraged at this nasty
turn of events. He bet a quarter. Jerry bumped to $1.25. Paul
dropped out and it went $2.25, $2.50 and $3.50. They were
down to three players.

	Down		*Up*		
Mac	5♡	A♡	A♠	3♡	K♠
Jerry		4♣	7♡	3◇	9♡
Frank		A♣	6♣	10♣	9♣

Mac was aware that if Frank didn't have a club in the hole,
his aces with a king would beat anything Frank held, so he
passed the buy. Jerry played pat. Frank glanced at his hole
card and passed the draw. The betting went 25 cents, $1.25,

$2.25, $2.50, $3.50. They all passed the third buy, and the final
bet again reached $3.50 as Mac, the high player, bet 25 cents
and the others raised $1 at each opportunity.

Frank had the flush.

Mac stayed out of the next hand as he went into deep thought
about the previous deal. He couldn't see that he had done anything wrong—just bad luck. It wasn't. Al would have passed the
first buy on 5, A, A, 7, 3. The need to see the action taken by the
other players was critical on this hand even if it meant giving
up one of the three chances for improving.

The last hand of the round of substitution was dealt. After the
fifth card, this was the situation:

	Down			Up	
Paul		6♣	5♦	J♣	A♠
Walt		7♣	6♦	9♡	J♠
Al		2♠	Q♠	2♡	9♣
Mac	4♡	5♣	7♡	K♠	K♡
Bill		2♣	10♠	A♦	8♣

Mac was proud of his kings, as if he were playing five-card
stud, and bet $1. Bill called. Paul raised to $2. Walt dropped out.
Al folded. Mac made it $3 and all called.

Paul pitched the J♣ and pulled the 2♦. Mac surveyed the
table and decided his kings were enough. Why waste $1? Bill
traded the 10 for a 4, which would have given Mac two pair.

	Down			Up	
Paul		6♣	5♦	2♦	A♠
Mac	4♡	5♣	7♦	K♠	K♡
Bill		2♣	4♦	A♦	8♣

Mac was high and the betting went $1, $1.25, $2.25, $3.25, $3.50.

They all stood pat for the $2 trade, and the betting again went
to $3.50 in exactly the same fashion.

They all refused the third substitution. The betting went a little differently this time:

Mac bet $1
Bill called
Paul went to $2
Mac noticed the change in rhythm but was unconcerned
He made it $3
Bill raised to $4
Paul made it $5
All called

Paul called low. Mac announced high and started to reach for the chips when he heard Bill say, "High; I have aces." Mac realized that in the earlier conversation he had practically announced that he only had kings, so Bill had acted the part of a weak 8 low. He had raised quarters to keep Mac from drawing. Mac found the remainder of the deck and looked at the top card—king.

They had concluded a round of three-card substitution, and Mac was now in the hole for $130. He held up his end pretty well for the next hour and a half. At 3 A.M. they started another round of substitution. It was agreed that these seven hands would conclude the game. Determined to get even, Mac plunged. He stayed on high-type hands that he would have folded in a high-only game, which is a common blunder of new high-low players. He held A, 2, 5, 6, 8 against 7, 4, 3, A showing. The 4s were dead, so the only card he could draw to beat his opponent, if the latter held any 7 low, was a 3. Even a 7 would not help. His opponent stood pat. Mac wilted and pitched the 8. He didn't improve, ending with a queen. His opponent had a 9 in the hole.

Mac had a flush-low combination—A♠, 7♠, J♠, 3♣, 4♠. He went for the flush, made it, and lost when an opponent pulled a full house.

It added up to $190 when they quit.

11

Stud Poker: Other Shapes and Forms

Standardization of the names of high-low poker games does not exist. As a result, you may find games which you have played for years described in this and other chapters with different tags

attached. New games are frequently tested, and when they are found to be adequate the originator puts a name on them. A month later he may find that the game he brought to life and named Baltimore Squeeze is called Grandpa's Twist in another part of the country. It doesn't matter much, as long as you know all the rules and conventions.

Seven-card high-low with a joker

This is a regular seven-card high-low game as described earlier, but is played with 53 cards. The joker may be used only as an ace or as a wild card in a straight or flush. It is a rather popular

game. To come out of this a winner, you must play a tighter game. Compared with ordinary seven-card high-low, a considerably stronger hand is needed to win. Kings over is a fairly strong holding in regular seven-card high-low. It isn't in this variation, because of the relative ease of bucking aces over, a straight, or a flush. Similarly, a stronger low is required because of the presence of the fifth ace. Two-way hands are much more common, since a low hand with the joker can easily include a low straight—joker, 6, 2, 4, 5, Q, 10 is a 6 low and a straight.

If you don't have the joker, stay only on strong lows and on very high hands for the first bet. An 8 low should never be your goal. If it comes along and looks good compared with other hands on the table, play it, but don't start with the 8 as an objective. Straight and flush-type starts are a little better than in regular seven-card high-low.

Low hole card wild

a. Last card "down and dirty"

This is seven-card high-low, but the lowest of your hole cards is wild and all like it in your hand are wild. An ace in the hole is treated as high in determining the wild card. Because of the relative ease of obtaining a two-way hand, the game is sometimes called "Hog It." Straight flushes are not uncommon. The high is rarely won with less than four of a kind. In fact, it usually takes a big four of a kind to win the high. Anything other than 6 in the low department is punk. If your low hole card is a 9 and you pair it, be calm. Your seventh card may be ruinous. Suppose you hold 9♠, Q♡ in the hole and 9♢, A♣, 4♣, 2♣ up. You have a perfect low and a straight flush for high in six cards, since both 9s are wild. You are not home yet. The seventh card may undercut the 9. Suppose you pull the 8♠. As the 8 becomes the wild card in place of the 9s, your hand converts to a 9 for low and three 9s for high. And that is some conversion!

You stay for the first bet on: three cards 6 or lower; low hole card paired; a pair of aces, kings or queens; three to a straight flush; or two to a straight flush and the remaining card as your low hole card.

b. Last card optional

The mechanics are the same as described above except that the last card may be dealt either up or down at the player's option. As you cannot be undercut, the raising comes a bit easier and the pots are larger. The hands are also a little stronger. It is sometimes dangerous to call both ways, for a perfect low may be tied. On the other hand, the last card may sometimes be taken "up" as a strategy play.

A, 3, 10, 6 showing may call for the last card up, merely as a show of strength, without a matched low hole card. This creates the impression of a perfect low. Such a play is not uncommon in a two- or three-man end game. Of course, the player must bet strongly to carry out the deception. It is pretty tough to call both ways against such an action and take the risk of being tied for low if you have A, 8 down and 8, 3, 10, 8, 7 up, which is four aces and a perfect low.

This form of deception works on the high side also. Assume you have the same hand—four aces for high and a perfect low. It is a two-man ending and your opponent has J♡, K♡, 6♣, 9♡ up. He bets very strongly on the sixth card, and when the seventh card is dealt he takes it up. He pulls the 7 of spades. He may be bluffing a straight flush or he may have it. You'll have to decide whether to try for the whole pot or be content with half the pot.

Six-card high-low

A junior version of seven-card high-low, this is played in an eight-man game when you don't want to fool with discards (or go into another deck). The cards are dealt—one down, one up and bet; up and bet; up and bet; up and bet; down and bet. An

8 low is excellent. Nine low is good. Two high pair should win the high. Any two pair is a good holding.

Any pair or any two cards 8 and below are good as a start. Nine and a smaller card is a satisfactory call on the first bet. Ace and a high card is optional. Fold any other pair of cards dealt.

Two-card substitution

This is also well suited for an eight-player game or to keep the size of the gamble down. It is the same as three-card substitution, except that only two substitutions are made. This eliminates a round of betting and the most expensive trade. The hands, of course, do not run as strong.

Push

This is a tantalizing little number in that you must make many decisions, and they are sometimes tough. Each player is dealt a hole card. Then the first player is dealt an up card. He either "keeps" or "pushes" the card to the player on his left. If he pushes, the first player is dealt the next card, which he must accept. The second player either keeps or pushes, and so on. When a man keeps, the top card is dealt to the next player. When the dealer pushes, the card goes out of the game. After the round of betting, a second card is dealt. You can push *either up card* or keep them both. This continues until after the fourth up card. When that round of betting is completed, a substitution is permitted, and it is dealt in the same way as described in Chapter 9. The substitution costs two and a half or three times the limit for the game and provides the only opportunity to dispose of the hole card. This is followed by a final round of betting and the declaration of high or low. This is a good eight-player game, as exactly 52 cards is the maximum that can be used.

Some features of this game may be noted: (1) This is a dealer's game and must be played for an entire round so that no player gets an advantage. Any game with substitutions where the second man sees the first player's action, the third player sees the result of the trade of both the first and the second players', and so on, gives the dealer an advantage. He sees the action taken by all of the preceding players, and when they take an up card, he sees what it is. Thus the game should be played for a full round. Another approach is to play a full round of any "dealer's game."

(2) You play for yourself first and for the table afterward. If you hold 6♡ down A♠, 4♣ up, and are dealt the K♢, you push it to the man on your left. The fact that this gives him a pair of kings is tough for the high players, but you have to play to win! Suppose you draw the Q♣ as your replacement card. Then on the next round you get the K♠. Now your hand is 6♡ down, A♠, 4♣, Q♣, K♠ and you must push a card. If you push the king, this will give the player to your left three kings, so you push the queen. In this instance, whether you push the queen or the king doesn't matter to you, so you play for the table. Furthermore, you may pull an ace and become a high player yourself.

(3) As in most high-low games, you should tend to prefer a low start rather than a high start. The ideal situation is to be playing low and have a high player to your right. The reverse is also good. In short, if you are not competing with the player who must push to you, he will sometimes "fatten you."

(4) One of the difficult problems that constantly arises in this game is the treatment of an 8. On the first and second up cards, I recommend pushing it. An 8 doesn't win the low often enough. On the third and fourth push you must decide on the basis of the apparent strength of the other low opponents and the exposed cards. If you are holding ace down and 2, 5, 8 up and receive a 6, but the 4s and 3s are all dead, you should hold the 8. You can only improve to a 7, 6, 5, and that isn't much of an improvement. On the other hand, if a preponderance of pictures has been exposed so that the 3s and 4s are live and there is some strong low competition, push the 8.

(5) There are two variations of push that are sometimes played. First, you can restrict the ability to push to the card dealt at that time, and this significantly reduces the range over which decisions are required. In the example above, you had a difficult problem of whether to push the 8. In this variation, you have no problem. As your only option is to push or keep the 6, you keep it.

Another variation requires that you pay when you push, with no charge when you keep. In a 10, 20, 30 game, the fee would be 10 cents each time you push. This doesn't change the game much, but it always creates problems. Did Charlie pay his dime? It's too much trouble.

Six-card push

This is played exactly like push except that in the end all players are dealt a sixth card down. The sixth card is in place of the substitution, and there is normally no charge for this card. The hands run strong and it permits two-way situations. As the sixth card is dealt down to everyone, it is not a dealer's game.

A variation is to deal the sixth card down, charge for it, and deal it only to those who pay.

Make your own hole card

Two cards are dealt down. When all players are ready, they turn up one of the two cards. After the bet, another card is dealt down, and either down card is turned up. The hole card is wild and any matching up card is also wild. After the first five cards are dealt and the bet is made, there is a substitution and a final bet. The substitution costs two and a half or three times the limit. The hands run very strong both for high and low. Any two cards 6 or below is an excellent start. Any pair is excellent since both will become wild cards by retaining one of them as your final hole card. As it frequently takes a 6 to win the low, a 7 and another low card is only a fair start. It is probably best to fold 3, Q. Two high cards should certainly fold. Don't play with poor cards merely in the hope of getting a pair which would give you two wild cards. Everyone has that opportunity—those starting with good as well as poor cards.

Baseball

This may be played either high only or high-low split. The cards are dealt as in seven-card stud—two down, four up, and the last card down. There are two wild cards: 3s and 9s. The 9s are free, and 3s dealt in the hole are also free. A 3 dealt up requires a payment by the recipient. When the dealer turns a 3 up, he stops and the player must decide, before seeing any additional cards, whether to stay and pay. I have seen all the variations described below on the charge for a 3:

a. The amount in the pot at that time

b. Half the amount in the pot at that time

c. Half the amount in the pot at that time up to a specified limit

d. Specified amounts—if it is a 10-, 15-, 25-cent game, the charge would be 50 cents for the first 3 dealt up, $1.00 for the second 3, $1.50 for the third, and $2.00 for the fourth.

e. Each of the methods described above can have further variations. The maximum amount that can be bet (the limit) may be changed to the amount that has been paid for a 3. In a quarter-limit game, if a player pays a dollar for a 3, the dollar becomes the limit that can be bet. A further variation is to permit only the player who has received the 3 and paid for it to bet that amount, while all others are restricted to the regular limit.

Of course, the player can refuse to pay for the 3, in which case he folds and is out of the pot. Furthermore, each player receiving a 4 up is dealt an extra down card. Should one of the hands pull two 4s up, he ends the deal with four up cards and five down cards.

The hands run very strong in baseball, and you must stay only when your first three cards show promise of developing a six low or a high four of a kind; nothing else is worth playing. If you play the variation where the limit is raised to the amount paid for a 3, you shouldn't even try for a 6, 5 low. It may seem crazy, but you should fold 6, 5, 2. Similarly, you should fold 3, 7, 8 unless the 7 and 8 are of the same suit and provide a play for a straight flush. The weakest hand you may stay on is Q, 9, A, which gives a play for four queens, four aces, or a perfect. If this is not improved on the next round by drawing a card to a perfect, a queen, an ace or a wild card, you should fold. If you start with three 7s, don't get excited. You may even choose to fold it. Four 7s losing an expensive pot to four jacks is a customary result, and if it is in high-low, it will really cost. As in low hole card wild, two-way hands are not uncommon— 9, 9, A, A, 2, 6, Q is four aces and a perfect.

Three-card monte

The stakes may be doubled in this game because there are only four rounds of betting and not much raising till the last two bets. Straights and flushes don't count. You are dealt one down and bet, a card up and bet, another card up and bet. Then there is a substitution at a price, and a final round of betting. Three aces is the best high, and 3, 2, A is the best low.

Three and two

The cards are dealt exactly as above except that there is no substitution round. It differs also in that only two cards are selected to make the hand. Thus, 2, A is a perfect low, and a pair of aces is the best high. The stakes should be doubled, as there are only three bets. Two-way hands are common and some exciting endings may come up. This may also be played with the ace as high only so that 3, 2 is a perfect low.

Five and three

The cards are dealt as in five-card stud—down and up, bet; up, bet; up, bet; up and final bet. Only three of the five cards are used in making up a high or low. Straights and flushes don't count, so three aces is the best high and 3, 2, A is the perfect low. Two-way hands are common in this game.

Seven-card high-low with a wild card

This is a variation of regular seven-card stud where one of the cards is designated as wild. The wild card should be a high card such as a 9 or a 10 rather than a low card. If a low card is made wild, it frequently does not improve a low hand. There should be a charge for getting a wild card up, and the player who receives it should be permitted to bet or raise the amount he has paid for the wild card. If it is a 5, 10 and 15 game, a charge of 30 cents should be made for an exposed wild card. The person paying 30 cents may then bet or raise 30 cents. He may choose not to pay for the wild card. In that event, he must drop out of that hand.

Should one person draw two wild cards up, he is charged double (60 cents) for the second wild card, and he can then bet or raise that amount. A wild card in the hole is the best bargain you'll ever get. It is free.

The hands run very strong. For the high side, a big full house is the normal winner and a six is ordinarily required for low. Your action should be geared to these targets unless the table suggests a different ending. If an opponent pulls two wild cards, the chance of your winning high with a full house is sharply reduced. Suppose a man raises strongly on 6, 2, 4 showing and next pulls a wild card—look out. Don't bother trying to pull a 6, 5.

Stud with a spit card

There are innumerable variations in which a spit card may be used. A "spit" is a card turned up in the center which may be used by all players in making their best hand. Here is one variation. The cards are dealt as in five-card stud. When the bet after the fourth up card is completed, the next card is turned up in the center and is a common card. This is followed by a round of betting. Then a substitution is permitted for the usual fee. It is a high-low game.

Another common variation is to proceed exactly as described above except that the center card is wild and all like it are wild. This makes very strong hands and heavy raising. Each player has at least one wild card. To create more raising, the wild spit card may be turned earlier—after the second up card.

Murder

This is a fast little number that has only five rounds of bets but builds very large pots. Considering the speed with which it is played, it becomes a stiff game. It is a two-card game with three substitutions. You pay for the substitutions the same as in three-card sub. You are dealt a down card and bet and then an up card and bet. This is followed by the three substitutions with a bet after each trade. Ace is a high card only and straights and flushes don't count. Consequently, a pair of aces is a perfect high and 3, 2 is a perfect low, but the game has a gimmick. A pairs of 7s takes the whole pot.

An inexperienced player usually goes for the pair of 7s, but this is frequently the wrong play. If the first card dealt down to you is a 7, your chance of making a pair of 7s is roughly 1 in 5 for four tries, so it is incorrect to play for this pair unless you have five or more players staying for the first bet.

In short, in a tight game, it is a bad gamble to play the 7 when you get one immediately. We will come back to the 7 shortly.

You stay for the first bet on a 2, 3, 4 or an A, with a 5, 7, or a K as an optional start when you have enough players in it. An ace is a powerful card in this game, as it can win the high with any decent added card as A, J or A, 9. A deuce or trey as your first card gives you a play for low or high. It can be paired on later rounds. A difficult problem is an A, 2 on the first two cards; you must decide whether to go for high or low.

It is sometimes correct to play the 7 in a loose game on the first card, but the beginner frequently makes this mistake. Pulling an ace for the second card, he continues to try for the whole pot; similarly with a low card, he plays for the 7s on later rounds. He does this even when another 7 is exposed, which greatly reduces the chance of pulling the pair. Once you get an A, 2, or 3 with a 7, it is a bad play to go for the whole pot.

12

Twin Beds and Roll 'Em Over

A number of high-low games are generated from good old-fashioned draw poker. Twin beds is probably the most exciting of them and will be studied in some detail. Others will be described in the next chapter. Each member of the draw-poker family can be played with or without rolling. The rolling adds lots of spice to the game as well as four rounds of betting and is highly recommended.

This game is well suited to eight players, which requires the use of fifty cards. Forty-five cards are used with seven players. The cards are dealt as in draw poker. In addition, ten cards are dealt into the center of the table and are arranged in two columns. One card from each column is turned up on completion of the deal and the man to the left of the dealer bets (or checks). After the first round of betting, two more cards are turned—one from each column. Then the second player starts the betting. This proceeds until all ten cards in the center are turned. After all the center cards are turned and after the fifth round of betting is completed, the rolling begins. Each player selects one of his five closed cards, and when all are ready, the card is turned. In the earlier part of the game, the first bettor for each round is determined by position at the table. Once the rolling begins, the high man bets first. The game proceeds in this manner until four cards have been rolled over by each player. The final round of betting is followed by the declaration of high or low or both ways. The last raiser declares first, and there is the usual jockeying for position. At the conclusion of a hand of twin beds the table looks like this:

Center Cards

Q♣ 6♠

5♡ 4♣

A♠ 9♢

9♡ 5♣

Q♢ 5♠

	Down		*Up*			
A	Q♠		7♡	10♣	A♢	2♣
B	3♣		6♣	K♡	2♠	K♢
C	Q♡		10♠	2♢	9♠	6♢

The hands are made in the following way. You take the five cards dealt to you and make the best high or low with either column. You are not allowed to mix cards from both columns to create a high or a low. You are permitted, if you call both ways, to make the high from one column and your low from the other column. On occasion both a high and a low may be made from the same column, and this is also satisfactory for a two-way call.

In the layout shown above, A holds queens full of aces in the left column. He also has a 6, 5, 4 low in the right column. To an opponent who does not see his hole card, he can have a perfect with a 3 as his final card or aces full with an ace. B's actual holding is a 6, 5, 3 low on the left side. A king in the hole would give him kings full, or a queen would give him queens full. C holds queens full of 9s. A 3 as his closed card would give him a 6, 5, 3.

There are nine rounds of betting in twin beds, and second-best hands can hurt badly. They can be especially painful when you get trapped with a strong low and a powerful high player who raise the limit at every opportunity. Ordinarily, the betting is on the mild side until the last two center cards are turned. From then on the betting is apt to be steep.

The first major decision is whether to stay at all. If you stay for the first bet and there is little raising as the beds are turned, you normally stay to see all ten center cards. This is the time for the next major decision. If you stay for the first roll, you ordinarily stay all the way. It is at this point (the turn of the ninth and tenth center cards) that you must toss in a small full house and even a bad 6 low. If you can't bear to concede a small loss on 6 low or a full house, you are a certain loser in this game.

A low full house will sometimes win the high. And I have seen 7 low win half the pot—but these are spot situations where the center cards are of a particular variety. Furthermore, hands of this type tend to yield small pots. If you play with a small full house, you can lose solidly. The odds are against staying on a weakish type of hand unless the board suggests that the hands will be weak and there is no raising.

Basically, you need a high full house or a good 6 low to win in twin beds. Consequently, you stay for the first bet only when such a hand has a reasonable chance of developing for you. For this reason 7, 7, 8, 8, K is a fair hand to start. It will likely develop a full house, but it is a full house that isn't too strong. On the other hand, K, K, 7, 8, 9 is a good first-round call. The chance of filling up isn't as good as the 7s and 8s, but if kings full come in, the prospect of winning is excellent.

Strong first-round calls:

   a. Any three cards 6 or lower regardless of the other two cards
   b. Four to a straight flush
   c. Three of a kind (you may make four of a kind)
   d. Any hand which includes a pair of queens, kings or aces regardless of the other cards

Optional first-round calls for small stakes, loose games, or in very high-ante games:

 e. Two cards to a perfect when one of the first two center cards is a third card for a perfect
 f. A pair of jacks, 10s or 9s when accompanied by a queen, king or ace
 g. Three in sequence to a straight flush
 h. Any pair which is matched with one of the center cards first turned
 i. An ace or king matched by one of the first cards turned
 j. Two pair where the higher pair is 9s or better

Here is a sample hand. The stakes are 10, 20, 30, with a 10-cent ante. No sandbagging. First two bets 10 cents, next two bets 20 cents, and later bets 30 cents. A pair on the table in the same column on the second, third or fourth turn of center cards permits a 30-cent bet.

Center Cards
4♡ Q♣

A	8♡	J♣	9◇	5♡	Q♡	A bust
B	3◇	6♠	6◇	8♠	J♠	Fair
C	A◇	10♣	10♡	5♠	9♠	Not much
D	J◇	5♣	8◇	Q♠	K◇	A bust
E	2◇	3♡	4◇	5◇	7♡	Good start, but the 4 in the center hurts as it helps others; holds 3 to a straight flush
F	2♠	3♠	2♡	J♡	K♣	Fair. As good as E on one side but not on the other
G	Q◇	A♣	7♣	7◇	10◇	Fair

G was the dealer, so A bet first. He checked. B bet 10 cents and all called except A and D. B bets on the second round, C on the following round, and so on.

On each of the following three rounds, two center cards were turned; a 10-cent bet and then two 20-cent bets were made by the first man, and all called. When the final two center cards were turned, the table was:

4♡	Q♣
K♡	A♡
3♣	4♣
9♡	6♡
K♠	A♠

B folded his 6s full on the fifth bet, which was 30 cents. The others called. They all rolled a card.

	Down				*Up*
C	A◊	10♣	5♠	9♠	10♡
E	3♡	5◊	2◊	4◊	7♡
F	K♣	2♡	3♠	2♠	J♡
G	Q◊	A♣	7♣	10◊	7◊

Looking at all the cards, let's review the situation. G has the high winner with aces full of queens. He need only worry about four kings, and he may be tied by another player with an ace and a queen. Either of these prospects is unlikely. C is the other high player, and, as he sees it, his prospects are good with aces full of 10s. The other ace might not have been dealt, but if it has, his hidden 10s along with the ace is fairly high. The queen in the right column may be trouble for C (and, of course, it is). F would fold his kings full, which cannot compete for high when a pair of aces is showing. However, he has a perfect low and stays, but E also has a perfect low.

G will always raise the limit. C may also choose to raise in the early rounds. On the fourth roll, when he sees the pair of queens or the third ace, C will realize he is probably beaten.

E and F will probably both raise. Only a deuce and a 3 are needed for a perfect, but with four players they will probably raise. They must get some money back, and it is unlikely that three players will hold a 2, 3 in their hands. Should that occur, they get only one-sixth of the pot, and raising will lose for them. The most likely prospect is that two players will have the perfect. In this case, they lose nothing by raising, as they will get back what they put in, but they hope to have no partner for the low. F is in a slightly stronger position to raise because he holds an extra deuce. In this hand G wins half the pot, and the two perfect lows each get a quarter of the pot.

If three players stayed for the final betting, it would be a bad gamble for a perfect low to raise. The two perfect lows would be getting less out of the pot than they put in for the rounds of betting with only three contestants.

I have been asked often how a particular hand should be rolled. In many situations, this is not easy to answer. It depends upon the impression you wish to create. Ordinarily you want to conceal your true strength, so you hold back a key card as your final hole card. The other cards may be turned in a variety of ways. At other times you want to present another posture and must roll your cards accordingly.

Suppose you have kings full and want lots of raising with this hand: K, K, A, 2, 8, and a K and 8 in one column in the center. You turn the deuce, a bet is made, you raise but no one else raises. If you think a possible low player is holding back on the raises because he is afraid of you as a contending low player, you should turn your king and an 8 early so that he might gain confidence in his low and raise.

In other situations, you may decide to bluff and turn your cards in an abnormal manner. Or you may have a medium sort of low which you want to play but you would like to cut down the raising. In this case, you turn your cards to show a potential perfect low early in the hope of stopping other low players from raising.

Of course, the hardest rolling problems and the exciting, challenging situations are the two-way hands. Suppose you have a 6, 5 low and as the play develops you find a contender who is beginning to "smell" like a two-way man with a perfect low and four 3s. You must turn your cards and raise to give the appearance of a perfect low. The object is to scare him out of a two-way call. You must convince him that he'll be tied for low on a perfect.

So when someone asks me how I would turn a hand, under such and such circumstances, I answer with a question: "What image do you want to develop and what kind of betting situation do you want to achieve?"

13

Pass the Garbage
and Its Kin

Pass the garbage

This is a draw-type game. Each player is dealt seven closed cards. This is followed by a round of betting which can be any amount and usually the limit is bet. After the bet is completed, each remaining player passes three cards to the man at his left and, of course, receives three cards from the person at his right. Each player next discards two cards, making his best high hand or his best low hand. Four cards are rolled, as described earlier, with a bet after each card. The declaration for high and low follows, although in this game the direction is obvious.

You are lost in this game if you do not recall the cards you passed and also the cards you received. If the player to your left stays in and you passed him 9, J, K, he must be holding at least one of these cards among the five he plays and cannot be a low player no matter what he turns in his early rolls. On the other hand, if you received three high cards from the player to your right, the chances are very good that he is going low.

The game is tricky and strange situations develop. Three players may remain for the rolling: B rolls a 9, C turns a 6, D turns a 5. At the next roll the hands become: B—K, 9; C—6, Q; D—5, A. But after the next roll, it might be: B—K, 9, 9; C—6, Q, 6; and D—5, A, 5. No true low is in the game, as all hands are paired. All of the hands look like a full house. (Four of a kind is possible but unlikely.) One of them might have played on two pair, intending to bluff a full house, and he would now be in a commanding position for the low. If they all have a full house, there is a real struggle from here on out. D is in the best situation, as aces full will win the high and 5s full will probably win the low. The others should not raise. D may try to call last, though his chance of winning the whole pot is slim.

On the final turn each player should avoid showing his three of a kind, which would certainly force him to declare first.

	Down		Up		
B		K	9	9	K
C		6	Q	6	Q
D		5	A	5	A

D might as well bet on his aces over showing, as he can't possibly get last call if the others know what they are doing. That is, if D checks, B and C should also check to force D to declare first. When D bets, B and C should merely call. If D declares high, B and C should call low. C will win with 6s full if he has it, and so forth. If D calls low, B must call high. He will have a "lock" if he has kings full. Otherwise his 9s full will beat 6s full but lose to queens.

The hands run very strong in this game and there is ordinarily a lot of betting. A high full house is good and a 6 low is usually required, but strange end situations are not uncommon, as in the case described above. As a consequence, some players go fishing. On two high pair they roll a high card. They must raise if the opportunity is present. If all players staying show low, they continue, hoping that two pair will really win the high. If another

player turns a high card which is lower than theirs, they have a choice of continuing the show of strength in an attempt to bluff the other player out. If the other high player stays for the second-round bet, the two high pair should fold. The object is to try to steal the pot but for a small investment—perhaps one big bet, or at most two bets. On the other hand, starting with two pair, they may find only high players calling the first bet and may end up taking the low side.

Six-card pass the garbage

The regular seven-card pass the garbage cannot be dealt with eight players. You may deal pass the garbage with six cards on such an evening, as this uses only 48 cards. Two cards are passed rather than three. The strength of the hands is rather sharply reduced. Any full house is excellent, and a high flush is also playable. A good 7 low (7, 5, 3, 2, A) becomes an excellent hand. There is more early bluffing. Suppose you play a flush. On the first roll another player shows a K♠ and bets and raises. On the next card he shows K♠, 8♡ and bets. If you have turned a high card so that he knows you are a high player, he is acting the part of a full house. You must decide whether he has it or is bluffing.

Twin beds, working sideways

The play is essentially as described in the previous chapter, except that you use the pairs of cards in the sideways direction to make your best hand, and you can use any of the five pair.

a.	6♡	J♠
b.	5♣	7◇
c.	Q♡	4◇
d.	8♠	9♠
e.	A♡	9♣

If this is the layout of the center cards, you can use any of the five pairs labeled a., b., etc. The hands do not run nearly as strong. With the particular layout shown above, a normal conclusion will be for a 7, 5 low and a spade flush to split the pot. Should one man hold A♠, 2♠, 3♣, 10♠, A◇, he has a reasonable two-way play on a 7, 5 low and an ace-high spade flush.

The center cards are turned so that the two cards in a pair are not shown at the same time. It takes three good cards in your hand to make a winner, and you stay for the first bet only when you have at least three good cards.

Twin beds, use one on each side

This is played like the regular twin beds, but in making your hand you may use only one card from each column to make your best hand. For a two-way play you can use one from each column for the low and a different pair (one from each column) for high. The strength of the hands runs in between regular and sideways twin beds. This game can present hands that are difficult to read because of the large number of combinations available. A full house is the more likely winner on the high side, and a 6 is usually needed for low.

Criss-cross

This is the most widely known of all the center card games and is probably the parent of them all. Five cards are placed in the center in the shape of a cross.

$$
\begin{array}{ccc}
 & 1 & \\
2 & 3 & 4 \\
 & 5 & \\
\end{array}
$$

They are turned one at a time, with the center card reserved for the last turn. This is followed by rolling as in any roll-'em game.

A low hand or high hand is made by using either the 1, 3, 5 or the 2, 3, 4 set with the five cards dealt to you.

A variation which creates strong hands, heavy raising and two-way calls is to treat the center card and all like it as wild. Another variation is to play the low card in your hand and all like it as wild.

Other center card games, use your imagination

Virtually any pattern of center-card arrangements may be used, although the games described above should provide enough variety to satisfy any taste. You make a circle out of seven or eight cards and turn them two at a time. Any two *adjacent* cards may be used in combination with the five dealt to each player. If you want stronger hands, use any three adjacent cards. An alternative is to build the circle but place one card in the center. Then the card in the center plus two adjacent cards in the circle may be used.

You may build a triangle and permit the use of any of the three sets of three cards. This may be varied by treating the number-one card as wild.

```
            1
         2     3
      4     5     6
```

Your artistic fancy may dictate a square:

```
      1     2     3
      4           5
      6     7     8
```

Use any of the four sets of three cards.

High-low draw

The cards are dealt exactly as in draw poker. A player may open on anything. After the draw and a bet, the cards are rolled in the usual fashion and the high man on the board bets first. This game comes up with some weirdies in the sense that the final contestants are all low or all high players more often than in any other game. Otherwise it offers little in the way of excitement. Its main purpose is as a steppingstone for new high-low players. It makes the conversion to twin beds a little smoother.

High-low draw with a spit

The game is played exactly as described above except that a spit card is turned, usually after the draw and before the rolling. The spit card is a common card available to all players. This permits two-way hands since a low and a straight or a low and a flush are possible.

Pick them up and roll 'em over

This starts as a stud game and ends as a roll-'em game. At the same time that the seventh card is dealt down, each player picks up his four exposed cards. He discards any two of his seven cards and a bet is made. When all players are ready, two of the originally exposed cards are rolled. Then the game proceeds as in pass the garbage.

14

Freddie
Rides Again

Al met Freddie at the service station Saturday morning. Fred had won the night before. He had drawn phenomenal cards and would have been a big winner if he had played the cards more skillfully.

Fred's car was being greased, and while Al was purchasing some gasoline they chatted about the game. Freddie was anxious for more action and wondered if the girls were going to set up a game that night. When Al's car was ready, he drove home to rake and burn leaves. As he methodically stacked the leaves, he thought over some of the hands of the previous night. Fred had certainly held good cards.

Early in the evening, in a hand of twin beds, Freddie seemed disinterested until the 4♣ and A♢ were turned as the seventh and eighth center cards. Fred looked around and asked whose bet it was. When it came his turn he raised. As the ninth and tenth center cards were turned, Fred showed his cards to Paul, sitting at his right, and mumbled, "This is going to be an interesting hand." After the fifth round of betting (first roll) only three players remained.

Center Cards

9♡ K♠

9♣ 5◊

8♡ 9♠

4♣ A◊

K◊ A♡

	Down				Up
Fred	A♠	K♡	3♣	2♣	6◊
Herb					3♠
Al					5♣

Fred had aces full of kings for high and a perfect low. What is more, the others would need four wired cards for a perfect low, and with the 9s spread on both sides of the board, four of a kind seemed unlikely. Fred figured he was bucking a 6, 5 or 7, 5 low and a smaller aces full. The betting and rolling were fast, with Al and Fred raising 30 cents at each turn and Herb raising 10 cents to reduce the size of the bet. The fourth roll came along.

9♡ K♠

9♣ 5◊

8♡ 9♠

4♣ A◊

K◊ A♡

	Down		Up		
Fred	A♠	6◊	2♣	K♡	3♣
Herb		3♠	J♡	6♡	J◊
Al		5♣	6♠	3◊	5♡

Al was high with 5s full and bet 30. Fred made it 60. Herb called. Al merely called. Oblivious to any danger, Fred called both ways. He felt that his original analysis was right. But Herb didn't agree with him. He was satisfied that he couldn't win the high with an ace in the hole. This gave him aces full of jacks, but Fred obviously had an ace in the hole. So Herb called low, hoping that Al had four 5s. Only a 5 down would justify Al's play all through the final rounds of betting.

Al did have four 5s! On the final bet he had tried to maneuver for the entire pot but couldn't. Herb had analyzed the situation properly. Only Freddie missed this one. A skillful player in Fred's seat would merely have called Al's 30-cent bet on the final round. In spite of the temptation, he would then probably settle for half the pot after hearing Al call high.

After a couple of small pots, one of which he won, Fred held Q, Q, 9, 9, 7 in twin beds. This is a pretty good start. As the cards were turned up in the center, a queen fell early and Fred was pleased with his full house. On the final turn of the center cards, a pair of kings was exposed.

Center Cards

6♡	J♣
Q◇	4♣
3♠	8♡
5◇	K◇
10♣	K♡

It is elementary in twin beds that you never buck an open pair with a lower full house. In this case, you must fold any full house lower than kings full. Even in a six-handed game, where twelve cards are unused, this is a clear-cut action. But Freddie couldn't bear to fold his pretty queens. He "fell in love" with his cards and lost an expensive hand to kings full of 8s. Occasionally queens full will win in this position. It requires that both kings be in the unused cards or, if they are in the game, that each person holding a king be without another pair. This is a pretty long shot and a very poor gamble. In this layout, it is even proper technique for a player holding a king to drop if his side pair is 4s.

Once Al left to get some cigarettes when he dropped out of a hand. He paused on the way back and noted that Freddie had played in twin beds on 5, 5, 6, 6, 10. This is against the percentages. While the chance of making the full house is very high, it will ordinarily not be enough to win the pot. But he made four 6s and that was certainly enough to take the high.

Then this hand came up. Fred held A♠, Q♣, Q◊, 2♡, 2♠. The center cards were turned two at a time with a bet after the turn of each pair.

4♣ 3♣
J◊ Q♡
A♡ 6◊
9♡ 8♣
A♣ 6♣

As Al thought about this one, he concluded it was one of the strangest hands of twin beds he had ever seen. Fred had been elated when the queen appeared on the second round. (Queens seemed to be glued to Fred that night.) He was even more elated when the pair of aces came up as the last two cards were turned.

The betting was a fast 30, 60, 90, $1.20. Four players remained for the rolling—one of them had bet and each of the others raised! They all rolled a card and the high man bet 30—raise, raise, raise. Again each succeeding player raised, which is unusual. They turned another card and the bet went to $1.20. The next bet reached $1.20 but not as rapidly. Paul pondered awhile and almost raised a dime. This was the pattern when the fourth card was rolled:

4♣ 3♣
J◊ Q♡
A♡ 6◊
9♡ 8♣
A♣ 6♣

	Down	Up			
Paul		10♠	K♡	7◊	6♠
Frank		2◊	J♠	10♡	J♡
Fred		2♠	Q♣	2♡	Q◊
Herb		9♣	5◊	K◊	9♠

Al surveyed the board and, strangely enough, there were probably no low players. Frank must have a jack in the hole. He had
bet or raised at every possible opportunity, and no other hole
card would explain his action. Herb had also played with excep-
tional strength and had four 9s. He would never have bet so
strongly all the way to the end on any other possible holding.
Paul could have a 7 low, but his play suggested that he had the
missing 6—four 6s.

Al watched Freddie, hoping he would see the situation, but he
realized that Fred wasn't concerned. He wasn't studying the
cards at all, quite satisfied with aces full. Frank was high and bet
30 cents. Fred still figured he had it and raised to 60 cents. The
next two called and Frank, who could have taken the last call,
didn't bother. There was no hope that the others would all call
high. He made it 90 cents. This time Fred just called, as did the
others.

Frank announced high. Al almost burst out with advice from
across the table but contained himself. Fred announced high.
Herb studied the situation. He, of course, figured Frank for four
jacks, but could he call low with four 9s? In the first place, it was
remotely conceivable that Frank had an ace in the hole, in which
case his four 9s would win the high. More important was the fact
that Paul had a 9, 7, low showing. As Herb's low was a 9, 8, he
would be beaten. From Paul's point of view, he (Herb) might
have an ace in the hole for an 8, 6 low. The silence was thunder-
ous as Herb pondered his problem. Fred finally started to look at
all the cards and realized his blunder. His 8, 6 was the best low
hand without any question.

Herb looked at Paul. Paul grinned contentedly. "I guess I
thought too long to be holding an 8 low," Herb said. In agony,
Herb cackled what sounded like high, conceding half the pot to
Paul. Frank turned the fourth jack. Paul showed the fourth 6 as
he sorted the chips. A strange hand indeed.

A while later in pass the garbage, Fred picked up this hand:
2, 3, 6, 6, 7, 9, K. He held the 2, 3, 6, 7, passing all the others.

Freddie might have folded this trash, but in playing it he should hold 2, 3, 6, 6. It is surprising how often this develops a full house by catching a 6 and a pair.

This play concedes the possibility of making a 7, 6 low, but the number of hands won on such a low is small indeed. On the next hand of pass the garbage, Fred made a perfect low. Bill bet, Fred raised, Al raised and Bill raised to $1.20. All the others folded. They turned a card.

	Down				Up
Bill					Q
Fred	6	4	2	A	3
Al					4

Bill bet, Fred raised, Al merely called, but Bill and Fred boosted it to $1.20. Bill turned another queen and the others turned low cards. Bill bet 30 cents; Fred bumped it to 60 cents; Al made it 70 and Bill went to a $1.00. And this was the pattern of all the succeeding bets.

Fred and Al both had the perfect low. They got back one fourth of the pot and put in nearly a third. Fred is oblivious to this little refinement. In a three-man ending with one high player and a prospective tie for low, it is murder for the low men to raise and end up losing for the hand. By holding each bet to 30 cents, the ante and early betting may be enough for the two lows to break even.

On the next hand Fred pulled 8, 8, 9, 9, 6, J, K. He held the two pair and received an 8 among the three cards passed to him. Al was the player to his left. Fred fancied his 8s full and bet them strongly even after Al turned a king, then a jack, a king and another jack. Al had a full house.

Fred forgot what he had passed to Al. An alert player knows what he has passed and in this situation would fold the 8s full. There is simply no hand, except a lock, that you have to play. When the player to your left turns K, J and you have passed these cards, the chance of a full house is so strong that you must fold a smaller full house promptly and take the small loss. You may be bluffed occasionally, but you'll show a profit in the long run.

As Al watched the last pile of leaves burn down to ashes, he couldn't restrain a smile. In spite of it all, Fred had won.

15

Hors
d'Oeuvres

Beware the little fat man

In the imagination of Hollywood or television casting directors, a gambling man is a smooth, trim character. He is tall and lean, tanned and well dressed. If he is a "good guy" type, he is clean-shaven and wears a light, tailor-made suit of the latest fashion. If he is a "heavy," he has a well-trimmed mustache and wears a dark suit. The professional gambler sleeps late and spends the day dealing poker hands and studying them. When the sun sets, he heads for the nearest poker game prepared for an all-night session.

It isn't so. Either casting directors have rarely touched a card or they think this is what their public wants. It is more likely that the winning poker player is a little fat man who runs a grocery store or the local gasoline station. You would never stop to look at him a second time. He is just an ordinary guy with a pedestrian vocation. But you can bet on this: If he runs a gas station, he runs it well. If he writes copy in an advertising agency, he is good at it. He is good at bridge or pinochle or chess if he plays these games. What he tries to do, he does well. (He probably wouldn't try ballet lessons.)

He may be a talker, but primarily he is a listener and a watcher. He sees and hears everything that happens at the table. When he sits down to play he forgets about his youngster's broken bike, the rough time he had at the office that morning, and his spouse's crying about how many times he has been out the past week. He has a good time at the table, but he concentrates on poker. He sizes up his opponents and knows their strength and their weakness. Much of his conversation is a cover for some action he is plotting.

The next time you play poker, pay some extra attention to that little fat man who wins so regularly; you will be surprised at the size of his bag of tricks. You may also want to try some of them yourself. You can learn more watching him for a few hours than you would from any other instruction you're likely to get.

Falling in love

It is sometimes a dreadful temptation to fall in love with your cards, as Freddie did when he held queens full (page 149). Remember, they are only cards. They will never respond. Play them when it serves your purpose, but on many occasions your grand design (which is to win) will be best served by severing your relationship with a particular set of cards. There are millions of combinations which can occur, and, except when you hold an absolute lock, the value of your cards may be measured only in relation to the cards held by others. What's more important, the relative strength of your cards is forever changing. You start with kings and jacks in a seven-man game of twin beds. You make a full house on an early turn of the center cards. On the final turn, a pair of aces appears in one of the columns. Fold immediately.

The odds are definitely against you, as the chance of aces full being present is something like 10 to 1 in a seven-man game.*

Suppose that you are playing pass the garbage and are dealt K, K, K, 10, 10, J, 4. You have a high full house. If you could change the rules for this one pot and pass only two cards, you could hold onto your full house and have an excellent probability of winning the high. Of course you can't change the rules, so you pass three cards to the player to your left. The proper pass is 10, 10, 4. This gives you your best chance of making a full house, in spite of the fact that there is a small danger in passing the pair of 10s. Now suppose that you don't catch the full house. Don't recklessly try to bluff a big full house. Of course, this may be the time to bluff, but in those few cases where it may be, your reason is not that you loved those cards you started with.

The saddest are these

Probably the saddest of all events for a poker bug is to stay in, make his best possible buy, and lose anyway. This really hurts. It occurs more frequently in the high-low games than in the "old-fashioned put 'em to sleep" poker games of yesteryear.

You'll never be able to avoid it completely. In three-card substitution, if you hold ace down and 7, 4, 3, Q up against only one potential low man standing pat with 2, 4, 5, 6 up, you have to stay and draw for a low. Only an ace as his hole card will beat you if you make a 7 low. Should you make the 7 and it turns out that he does have the ace down, console yourself with the fact that this was one of those situations where you had to stay. Just

* Twin beds—seven players: This uses 45 cards. The seven unused cards will include the two aces once in 35 hands. In this case, kings full will win. In approximately one out of three pots, one ace will be in an opponent's hand and one unused. You will win when that opponent doesn't hold another pair among the other seven cards in his hand and in the column with the two aces, or if he folds before he sees the pair of aces in a column in the center of the table. In the remaining cases, almost two out of three times, both aces will be dealt. You win with kings full if *both* players don't have an added pair (a very small chance) or fold early.

be sure that you don't play this next one: ace down and 7, 6, 4, Q up against two potential low opponents with 7, 4, 3, A and 6, 4, 2, A. Now the situation is completely different and you should fold. In this case, it is very easy to make your best buy and be a loser. To start with, you can make only a 7, 6 low, and this can easily be beaten. Second, neither of your opponents can have a straight. And most important, you are now bucking two men, not one. The exposed cards will tell you a lot about your opponents' prospects and your own chance of improving. You also know quite a bit about the style of your opponents. So sum it all up and make your play, but make a real effort to avoid the second-best propositions. If you run into them often, you are probably staying in too many pots.

It might have been

You fold in seven-card high-low at the fifth card holding 8, Q down and A, 6, K up. When the next card is dealt you note that you would have gotten a deuce. On the seventh card you impatiently wait until it is over and then learn that the guy two spots to your left pulled a five. Had you played, you would have made an 8, 6 low. The pot was won by a 7, but you hurriedly reconstruct the fact that he wouldn't have made the 7 low if you had played. He would have been paired on his last card. After a little more post-morteming you announce, "I folded a winner."

The next hand is push. You start with the A◊ down and get the 2♣ up and keep. You next get the Q◊, and of course you push it. You receive the 6◊. Your card on the next round is the 10◊. This time you ponder it awhile, inspecting the cards on the table. You finally decide to play for low rather than a diamond flush and pull the 8♣ in place of the 10◊. Your next card is K◊. You push it and draw low diamond, making an 8, 6, but you wind up losing to an 8, 5. Seeking sympathy, you explain to the neighbor on your right that you held a diamond down and could have made a flush. He yawns.

Don't torture yourself. There are thousands, perhaps millions of combinations of cards and situations that might occur. Make the action that you judge to be correct over the entire span of possible events. And please note that the man at your right might not have pushed all those diamonds if you had decided to play for a flush. Why shouldn't he be bored?

Do you remember all the times you folded early because you seemed to be going nowhere? When you drop early in the play and it ends up as the correct action, you don't tell your neighbor that you wouldn't have made anything. He would be worse than bored; he might think you were nuts. You must hold good tickets in a high-low game to play once the betting gets stiff. You get only half the pot and ordinarily that means you're only getting around 1½ to 1 odds for the entire pot and around 2½ to 1 from the fifth card in stud or substitution or the point where the rolling begins in twin beds. You have to win often when you play to the end in a high-low game. So occasionally if you fold a hand that would have been a winner, don't be too concerned. It has to happen from time to time or else you're not folding often enough. You don't expect to win every pot you play to the end and, similarly, you cannot expect to be correct on every drop-out.

Sick, sick, sick

Have you met this character? He has K, J up in seven-card stud and a king falls to his right. He whacks the table with his paw: "My card." Then he inspects his right-hand neighbor's cards and wants to know why in the hell the guy stayed on such trash and "drew *my* king." He feels he held the mortgage on it. On the next hand, which is three-card substitution, he holds four low cards (6, 4, 3, A) and a picture, and is desperately trying to pull a 2, 5 or 7. On the first trade, he pulls another picture. On the second trade, he pairs. On the final trade, he pulls another picture, but the man to his left gets a deuce. This time he announces that if Paul, who is in front of him, hadn't folded he would have made a perfect. And what right did Paul have to fold with a potential 8 low? Paul grunts, "You play your cards, and let me play mine."

This sick character is more concerned about developing "crying points" than he is about winning. He enjoys this business. He is more interested in what he would have gotten than he is in what he has pulled. The hands where he gets the card he needs because one of the others has folded don't count. There is nothing to cry about.

I love to play against this type. He enjoys losing, and as I want to win, we are all happy. Watch him carefully, for he scans each card as it is turned, ready to pound the table to score "crying points." He sometimes slips and gives his hole card away.

In search of the holy grail

This expression has a wide application, but it seems to fit best in three-card substitution. It is obvious when you go "grailing" in this game. If you hold 6 down and A, 8, J, Q up and stay for the trading in the hopes of drawing two low cards, you're out on a grail job. You have to make two good pulls out of three, and the chances are you are heading for the poorhouse.

There aren't many circumstances where grailing makes much sense. First, if you don't improve on the first trade, get out. Second, be sure that if you buy what you're after you'll win. Third, the cards that you need must be real live. Finally, you should recognize that you're embarked on a grail job, and play accordingly. If you hold 7, 5, 2, J, 10 and the aces are dead, three of the 4s, two of the 6s and a 3 are exposed and you play it, you're not grailing at all; you're committing suicide. It is hardly ever correct to grail for an 8 low. That introduces the next item on the list of appetizers.

That awkward 8

You can win the low side with an 8 in some of the games. Of course, we are not concerned with twin beds, pass the garbage, or the multicard or wild-card games, for in these an 8 hardly ever takes the low. The games where an 8 is a problem are seven-card high-low, push in its various forms, and three-card substitution. We have discussed the 8 in earlier parts of the book, but it is important enough to warrant some repetition. In push and three-card substitution, an 8 isn't worth a great deal unless the board seems plenty weak. Of course it wins sometimes, but it is poor percentage to go for an 8 as an objective. The odds against it are strong. There are 8s and there are other 8s. In the three-card sub, the difference between 8, 7, A, 2, K and 8, 4, 2, K, A when the trading starts is enormous. An 8, 7 low is only a step removed from no low at all. When a prospective 8 low comes along in these two games, fold unless there is a specific justification for playing it.

In seven-card stud and two-card substitution, the value of an 8 steps up a little. It is a fair low in those games, where it isn't much for push or three-card sub. It is now a card you can play, but don't be surprised if you make the 8 and lose. And for goodness' sake, don't raise with it unless the others seem awfully weak for the low.

To sum up, an 8 is awkward. In most of the stud games, it must be played carefully and conservatively.* Fold it against strong opposition and toughen your hide, for there may be some comments. The comments will come from the habitual losers.

Trouble ahead

You'll sometimes play high-low games with eight players where it is possible to run out the deck. In a loose three-card sub game, if there is a lot of substitution in the final rounds, this happens. It may also occur in seven-card stud. You may choose not to play games where this can arise, but it isn't necessary. It is necessary that you recognize that it can happen and set up a method of handling the situation if it should come up. There are two satisfactory ways of completing the hand. One way is to go into a second deck for the extra few cards needed. A second is to assemble *all* the discards at the point where you have run out of cards,

* An 8 low is excellent in six-card stud.

shuffle them and proceed. Either method is fair to all parties, provided it is agreed upon in advance. Once a method is accepted, it is not necessary to go through the ritual each time the players assemble, but if a new player joins the game you must be sure that he knows the rule you choose to follow before the game starts. This is ordinarily a problem only in an eight-handed game. It sometimes adds a little to the game, for a player might stay at the end when he sees that he is going to get a crack at the other deck or the discards.

Don't be bashful

Playing in a new group, I heard the dealer announce three-card monte. I pulled some good cards and bet strongly. I held 2, 4, 5, which is a lock for low in three-card monte against 6, 2 up. He held a 3 down and beat me. It turned out that we weren't playing three-card monte at all; we were playing three-two with a substitution.

The high-low poker games are infants in the great family of card games, and there are no standard names. When you sit in a new group of poker players, ask lots of questions. Don't depend on the names with which you're familiar, and don't be bashful. Be sure you know what you are playing before you start tossing chips into the center of the table.

Handling the two-way hand

This is where the big money comes or goes. You don't get many cracks at both ways. In the games where you wind up with five cards (substitution, regular push, pass the garbage) the prospect doesn't arise. In seven-card stud, six-card push, low hole card wild and all of the center card games, a two-way possibility may come up. You'll get maybe one or two hands in an evening where you have the possibility of a two-way call. When you get the opportunity it is a disaster if you call it wrong—by missing both ends of the pot when you have it, or calling both ways and not having it.

I recently saw a real boner pulled in a six-card push game. It was a four-man end position when one of the players suddenly dropped out. A potential two-way player had a straight and a 7 low and was bucking a high player and a low player. The high man had not bet strongly. The low opponent had laid it on at several points in the proceedings and showed a possible 6. The two-way man misjudged the situation; he concluded correctly that he didn't have it both ways. But he went low. Two pair took the high unopposed. The low man had the 6. The potential two-way player got nothing, having called low. He had called against the player who had been betting strongly rather than against the obviously weak high player.

Two-way possibilities are often difficult to judge in a strong game. The good opponent sometimes feels it coming and will raise and otherwise confuse the situation to try to prevent the two-way call. There are no easy prescriptions for success in this department. If you play the high-low games well, you'll handle these problems well also.

Several years ago I stumbled into a high-low game played with pot-limit stakes. This is a strange game indeed. I had never heard of high-low games played in this manner and never expect to see one again. It was an odd game in other respects. All the players, except me, were young men around twenty-one or twenty-two. They were all single, with no family obligations. In spite of the fact that the income of each of them was perhaps half of mine, their concern about the dollar was about a fourth of mine. The pots were huge. The host for the evening lived in a roominghouse and the game was played on the bed in his room as the players sat about the edges of the bed. Mountains of green were strewn about and especially in the center of the bed. This was nothing new for these young men. They were all just out of college, starting their careers, and they were accustomed to such surroundings. To me it was strictly Damon Runyon but without the colloquialisms.

I won a giant two-card-substitution pot both ways. This is not just unusual; it is almost impossible. I remember only the ending:

	Down		*Up*		
A		7	A 5	4	
Me	10	2	3 4	A	
B		2	3 5	7	

All the potential high players had dropped. The opponents stood pat with the cards shown for the second substitution. Before the final trade, I had A, 2, 3, 4 up and a 10 down. The play of both opponents suggested that they had lows but either could have had a pair. I pitched the 10 on the ground that I couldn't be hurt for high and might improve for either high or low. I pulled a 7. Two aces had been folded earlier. A made a large bet; I merely called instead of raising; B called. I had an inspiration that I could get it all if A announced first and declared low, so I decided not to raise. He did announce low. I now had the whole pot, provided B didn't have a pair. I called both ways, satisfied from earlier actions that B had a low. He had a 4. This is the only time I have seen a two-way call in a five-card game.

Watch your position

In a coed poker game, as the evening was nearing an end, I was down about three dollars and was being teased. Playing along with the gag, I engaged in some banter and at one point noted that in a sense I was down four dollars because my position was worth about a dollar. This met some raised eyebrows, so I explained. The player to my right was a tricky character who raised and raised and raised. The player to his right was also a "big" bettor and a strong man to boot. On the other hand the player to my left rarely raised. This seating arrangement was a big plus value for me. I could call in comfort with little expectation of raises behind me. And I could make my decisions after the raises so frequently made to my right. Poker is a game where uncertainty plays an important role, and from where I was situated at the table, an element of the uncertainty was removed.

You can't always seat yourself in the ideal position. When you are the host it is not proper poker etiquette to set out name plates. But every now and again you can cash in on where you settle your tail for the evening. When you arrive at a game, suppose there are five players already seated. They'll be busy dealing some hands of showdown or blackjack while waiting for the others to arrive, and there will be two or three vacant seats. Without any fuss, head for the seat in back of the big bettor or the strong, tricky player. If you are fortunate enough to find yourself also in front of the guy who would just as soon cut the stakes, that is even better. He is the guy who hates three-card substitution. He prefers criss-cross to twin beds. Your position for the evening is not the most critical factor, but it is important enough to warrant some attention as you sit down to start a game.

Bake me a cake

If you have a sweet tooth, as most of us have, you are fond of a good slice of cake. It mustn't be too moist, or too dry, or too heavy, or too light. You certainly know that the quality of the ingredients is a critical factor. So it is with poker. An assortment of the right ingredients will make it a better game and increase the enjoyment of all.

These are the ingredients suggested for high-low games. First, there should be three levels of betting—for example, 5, 10 and 15 or 2½, 5 and 10. Second, sandbagging in any form should be acceptable. To play otherwise deprives you of a beautiful tool. You wouldn't dream of insisting that a chocolate layer cake be prepared without butter. Remember that the player who attempts a sandbag is taking a risk that there will be a bet or raise behind him. In high-low games the elimination of sandbagging can really be silly. Suppose you hold an 8 low in seven-card stud. A high player to your right bets and you call. A player with a "sevenish"-looking hand to your left raises. The high player also raises. When the bet comes back to you it is sort of crazy not to be allowed to raise the minimum to kill a raise. Yet, if you disapprove of sandbagging, you cannot kill a raise as you have once passed the opportunity to do so.

Another rule which I suggest is to scale the betting by the round rather than the presence of an open pair. The first round (the first and second in some games) should allow the small bet. The next two (possibly three rounds in twin beds) should permit the intermediate level bet, and all subsequent rounds should permit the highest possible bet. This should be without regard to the presence or absence of an open pair. It should be apparent from the preceding pages that the low player has an edge. Yet when a player gets an open pair, the betting goes to the limit. This is sort of topsy-turvy.

A couple of years ago I played in a game that I really admired. All the players were strong, remarkably strong, for a neighborhood game, and they had a number of good conventions. One of them was simultaneous declaring of high and low. This was discussed earlier and I urge that it be tried at least as a variation. There was another good rule that they applied vigorously—no light play. I find it most annoying to play in a pot where a couple of guys are light from the very beginning. In high-low games the betting and raising are sometimes fast and complicated. It is very easy to make an unintentional mistake, such as tossing in some chips from a light stack instead of adding to it. Furthermore, it is always necessary to have a general notion of the size of the pot, and this is sometimes difficult when some money that belongs in the pot isn't there. Also, splitting the pot can be a nuisance with light players. It is not that I don't trust the guy. I wouldn't play in a game where there was even a remote chance of dishonesty. The point is that light playing creates confusion and is an imposition on the other players.

I don't think it is necessary to banish playing light entirely. If a player runs out of chips toward the end of a pot, it is all right for him to complete the last round or two playing light. It does hurt to cash that sawbuck, and, of course, it is ordinarily the loser that is light. But playing light from a very early round of a hand all the way to the end should not be allowed. I find it particularly obnoxious when a big winner runs out of chips and plays light. Light play should be a privilege accorded only to losing players. A winner should be required to cash that big bill. I have been waiting for years to witness an end position with two or three players left, all of them playing light, and running out of chips. I haven't seen it yet.

Bury this one

This bit on a draw-poker hand doesn't belong in the book in one sense, but the temptation is too great. It is a poker story* which I have run into more than once. The limit was $25. There were a number of raises before the draw, and the pot was in the $300-plus department. Each of the two contenders (other participants at the draw folded later) drew two cards. Our hero, in with three queens, pulled another queen and an ace. After a series of $25 raises, he folded, announcing that his opponent's four kings and ace kicker beat his four queens. As the story goes, our hero went through a step-by-step analysis, explaining what each raise meant. His opponent's final raise meant four kings and an ace kicker, and now a quote:

> With all that money in the pot, and four Queens in your hand, wouldn't you have tossed in another twenty-five dollars? You probably would have. But to Dundee the old poker adage, "Never throw good money after bad," was second nature. Once he knew "Straights" Fowler had him beat, he threw in his hand without a whimper.†

You're damn right I would call for $25. At this point there was around $700 in the pot. The odds were 28 to 1! Dundee's judgment of what each successive raise meant in increased value had

---

* *Poker According to Maverick*, pp. 65–68.
† *Ibid*, p. 68.

to be *exactly* right. Also there was always the possibility that
Fowler might be on a bluff. Maybe Fowler knew that he (Dundee) was enough of an ass to fold four queens and just continued
raising until Dundee's analysis brought him (the opponent) up
above Dundee's holding. Call for $25 and end the baloney. Or,
better still, call on the previous round. But no, on his previous
bet Dundee expected to win that big pot and just had to get another $25 of Fowler's money. At that point the situation was solid
enough so that expert Dundee could raise, but Fowler raised
back just one more time and now the house came tumbling down
on a $700 pot. And all because of one more raise.

This little episode is preceded by a tidbit* where two guys
were raising like crazy because they were both bluffing and finally
one of them called. As they were both bluffing, the "experts"
noted that the raising should have gone until one of the players
folded. A pair of deuces won the pot.

In short, if you are bluffing on a bust you must continue raising
or go out. (This part is good advice.) And if you're betting on
four queens, you continue raising until it is "time" to go out. Play
them both the same way. After umpteen raises you'll *know* that
your opponent has exactly four kings, not four jacks.

I call on four queens in draw poker.

When Mac makes the switch

I have tossed some minor bombs at old-fashioned poker, but
mainly for the shock effect. In truth a strong poker player in the
older games will make a good high-low man. An inept player will
find the high-low games particularly bruising. The sound player,
after a period of accommodation, will find his advantage over the
less skillful even greater, for the range of decision and deception
is increased. The gulf between the able and the inept is widened
as there are more things to do, more to know, and more variations
to handle. If our friend Mac of earlier chapters is as good as he

* *Ibid,* p. 65.

claims, he'll be a terror at high-low in spite of his smugness and his smelly cigar.

But high-low games need never replace the standard forms of poker when it comes to big money. For the big gambling games, you can play high-low or the regular games. If you choose to play no-limit, table stakes or pot limit, you have to play the regular games. The high-low games don't fit. But high-low games fit any limit stakes quite well.

At small stakes such as 5, 10, 15 cents or even 10, 25, and 50 cents, the standard games are sad. The element of bluff via the big bet is completely removed and it is almost mechanical, especially for the seasoned expert.

16

The Many Faces
of Poker

The earlier pages of this book mainly covered the technical aspects of poker. Now we turn to the area of bluff, strategy and deception. A technically solid player will be a winner in the long pull in an average game, for the quality of play in the average poker game is remarkably inept. In a strong game, the technically sound player, who is weak in deception and strategy, will find the road a bit rough. A high-stakes game is not necessarily a strong game. I would venture a guess that nine in ten regular poker games are soft, but the solid technical player will win even more in a soft game if he also plays a good psychological game.

The high-low games offer a wide panorama for strategy plays. In draw or five-card stud, unless played at table stakes or pot limit, the range for deception is remarkably limited even at fairly high-limit stakes. You open on three of a kind for $5 in draw and two players call. You check into a one-card draw after the cards are dealt. He bets the limit—$5 or even $10—so what. If you are playing table stakes and he bets $100, you have a nasty problem. On the other hand you can ram it right back at him—you check, he bets $100, and you bump to $500 or "tap" for even more. In limit stakes, however, it is a lot of nothing. You check, he bets $10 and you raise $10. What is his problem? If he has a decent hand, he calls. You bluff rarely in a limit-stakes game because the prospect of success is so slight.

In the high-low games bluffing in the sense of causing an opponent to fold is a small part of the deception-strategy department. A player does not merely decide whether to stay or drop; he must decide on announcing high or low. He must decide which card to push to his neighbor in some games or which card to pitch in other games. In the substitution games a player sometimes must make a decision to go for a high or a low, and once the decision is made there is no recovery. You try to influence his decision by your betting, your demeanor and your conversation. On the final round in twin beds you jockey in the betting to call first (not last) to create a particular posture. This time it is the posture of a man who holds a solid hand, wants the pot as big as possible, and doesn't care whether he calls first or last. The purpose is to influence a potential opponent to call in the opposite direction. It is plays of this kind, the ability to spot the situation and to execute the play successfully, that distinguishes the expert at high-low games from the mere technician who knows when to fold and when he has a probable winner.

Command of the table

This is the ability to understand what is happening: who is trying to do what and why. Don't expect perfection, for poker is a game of uncertainty. But in many hands of push, make your own hole card, substitution and others our friend Al can tell you what each player holds as his down card. He can guess what each player is trying to accomplish. He is right most of the time. The other night a hand of make your own hole card was dealt in the game with the girls. Marie, Al's lady, was puzzled at the fourth card. The others were waiting impatiently. She was not ready to turn up one of two down cards and she was delaying the game. From across the table Al said, "Turn the ace." She stared at him. She turned an ace!

In the men's game at the seventh card in a four-man ending, Bill smelled out a situation where the low players were weak. He had 7, Q, 2, A up and 7, 5, J down. The jack as his final card had ruined his hand, but he raised. Al to his right also raised and declared first. Al called low. The two others called high. Bill, with not much prospect either way, called low. Al said, "You've got it. I have a busted flush, but it just looked like no genuine low."

Bill grinned. "That's why I raised. I only have jack for low."

Al looked at his cards. "Jack what?"

"Jack, 7."

Al looked again. "Beats my jack, 8."

They had both spotted a no-low-player situation and banged heads. Of course, had either of them spotted it earlier, he might have succeeded in bringing it off. How do you smell out the situation? It is impossible to describe. You know all the cards that were folded; you know the style of the other players; you watch and listen. Freddie is staring at Bill's cards, not Paul's; Frank appears to be counting the diamonds; Mabel is fingering her cards, ready to fold when the bet reaches her; Bill, a strong player, is studying the size of the pot and from the looks of him is considering dropping out. If you are oblivious to these tidbits, you don't have command of the table. If you observe them but your batting average on interpretation is low, you don't have command of the table .

Know your man

Each player has his own style, his own strength, his own weakness. Most players react in their own private way in particular situations. Sit down some balmy fall afternoon and record the style, characteristics, strength and weakness of each player in your crowd as an exercise. How do they play when they are winning? When they are losing? In the last round? Can they be bluffed? How do they each play an 8? And so forth. You may be amazed at the knowledge stored between your ears that you haven't bothered to use.

Take this situation. In pass the garbage you get some real old-fashioned bluffing problems. The reason is that a player shows as a high man at an early point where only a small investment has been made and a large investment is required to play it down to the end. In a four-player ending Freddie turned a 9. You have a busted full house, kings and queens and a 10. You turn a king. The other two players each turn a 4. Should you try to bluff the big full house? Not against Freddie. He knows that he has a full house and you are not going to push him out. There is a bridge expression that fits this situation: "You can't psyche a palooka." In poker it is hard to bluff an inept player. Try Al with the same problem. You can bluff him. He'll fold a full house against some guys. Against this type of player he might add a comment, "I was going to run one." No need to let the solid citizen know that he folded a full house. But he may also fold in pass the garbage against a player who bluffs occasionally.

Freddie is prepared to raise on K, Q, 8 up in seven-card. You are on an intermediate hand and don't want the raise. He probably has two high pair. Bill, to your right, has bet first with a pair of 6s; Freddie is at your left. As you toss in your chips you glance about. "Where the hell are the other two 6s?" Freddie just calls. Bill wanted a raise and would have laid on another one, for he is playing low. You stopped Fred from raising and caught Bill by surprise because it happened fast. Otherwise Bill would surely have let Freddie know by some means that a 6 was turned earlier. Bill gives you daggers, but says nothing because he pulls the same stunt. It is all over Fred's head. He doesn't know a 6 was turned. He doesn't see Bill's glance at you. He may not even know why he didn't raise; he just changed his mind.

Should you try this little maneuver on Al? He might burst out laughing. For Al you use a scalpel. For Freddie a mallet. Fred won't see the beauty of a subtle play. Against Al you don't exactly deceive. He knows what you are capable of doing. You create a problem for him and hope that he'll go wrong. It is a play that sometimes needs preparation and timing. Something like this:

It is three-card substitution after the fourth up card. You hold a K down and 5, 5, Q, J up. Your 5, J, K are live. They must be live or the play is hopeless. The beauty is that you frequently end up winning this sort of hand naturally and you start building the pot in advance. You raise and if it comes around again, you raise again. What does the play do to Fred? Nothing; he proceeds to play his own cards. But now consider Al. Even though he knows you might not have two pair, he will have some rough problems to face. He knows, of course, that your cards are live. Suppose he has A, A, 7, 4, 3. You have made it a little tougher for him to play high. If he has A, A, 7, 4, 10, he'll throw the 10, but if he buys a deuce he has the same problem at the next round. Suppose he has a four flush, goes for it and makes it, but you discard the queen and buy a third 5. You bet and raise and raise. Now if his flush includes four low cards, he will consider breaking it to go for low. If the low cards he needs are live, he'll be even more tempted. It would never occur to Fred to toss the Q and go for low holding Q, 7, 5, 4, A of hearts.

Assume Al has a pair of 10s when you first raise on 5, 5, Q, J showing. He'll probably fold, but if he pays the raise you still have a good chance of winning because your cards are live. If he has two short pair—10s and 6s—he is also in a rough spot. He knows you have a good chance of making two higher pair or possibly already have it. He can look forward to three more expensive rounds of betting plus three costly attempts at a full house. He might easily conclude that it isn't worth the gamble.

Your timely raise on this particular set of cards has made it rough for high opponents. Where no problem existed, you have created one. Where they had a small problem, you have converted it to a hard one. But this is so only for a perceptive opponent.

Change of pace

As all baseball fans know, a successful pitcher is one who mixes 'em up. He keeps the batter off balance; he keeps him guessing. He throws fast balls, slow balls, knuckle balls and curves; they come inside, outside, high and low. He has no specific sequence. A sinker sometimes comes after a slow ball high and inside. At other times it is thrown after a fast curve to the outside corner. Should the batter guess what a particular pitch will be and where it will come, the little white pellet will go for a merry ride into the bleachers, and the pitcher will soon find that his services are no longer in demand.

The same is true of the quarterback in football. He keeps the defense off balance. He must not repeat the same sequence of plays repeatedly or he'll find the defenders swarming all over him. This is true of any strategy game. Even a simple odd-even or matching game is a strategy game. These are very simple two-player strategy games. From your point of view you must never resort to a sequence which your opponent may guess. You must create random actions by tossing or shaking your coins. In the meantime, if your opponent arranges his coins for matching, you attempt to guess his sequence.

Poker is also a strategy game. It is a complicated one and the penalty for being outguessed is severe. If you always raise in a particular situation, if you never are bluffed, if they run like

hell when you raise, if you tend to drag nonchalantly on a cigarette when you make a good draw, if you suddenly become alert
whenever your situation improves, if you're a talker and shut up
when you hold a lock, if you take any of a number of other
actions in a consistent pattern, you are in trouble. The chances
are that you pay for it.

In the situation described just above, where you played the
pair of 5s as though you had more in substitution, all of your
actions and conversation should be about the same as they
would be if you had a third 5 in the hole. If you are a talker,
keep talking. If you are the strong silent type, don't start bab-
bling.

You must first study yourself and, when you have mastered
your own weaknesses, make a concerted effort to learn the weaknesses of your opponent. While you are taking this little course
in strategy, give 'em the old change of pace. Take a couple of
hands early in the play—but only when you have fairly good
prospects—and play them a bit differently. Raise when you
would only call and call if you would raise. You may play the
final bet in these hands naturally. Only a couple of hands of
this kind of stuff are needed each night—no more. After a half
dozen nights of this kind of carrying on you'll be amazed at the
results. The good results will not come on these two hands.
They'll come in other ways. If you're the conservative type of
player, you'll find the pots you win a little bigger. If you're the
wild give-'em-hell type, you'll find yourself stealing a share here
and there.

Probably the most common failing in the strategy department
is overbluffing. This is strictly a losing proposition. You don't
win many pots bluffing, and there is such a thing as too much
advertising. Of course, the ideal state of affairs is to have a
reputation as a cagey, suspicious character. Then you can play
them right down the middle. You act the part of a carnival
swindler when you're holding a 6 low. They will call on a 7 or
even a bad 8.

Let's take a short diversion here to explain what is meant by bluffing. You can't make that $1,000 bet in a 25-cent limit game. In general a bluff is where you represent your hand, by your betting or otherwise, as strong when it is truly weak. When you make a $1,000 bet on a busted flush in a draw poker, it is made in the hope that your opponent will leave the field of battle. In the high-low situations you represent your hand as stronger than it really is in an effort to get your opponent to act in a manner favorable to you.

In three-card substitution you hold 7 down and A, 3, 5, Q up. On the first trade you ditch the queen and pull a 7. You now show A, 3, 5, 7, which certainly looks like a powerful low, but actually you hold a miserable pair of 7s. It is a four-man ending and two of the players are battling for high. Your only low opponent sits to your left. He also pitched an up card and pulled an 8, giving him 8, 7, 3, 2 up. Your objective is to get him to dispose of the 8. If you raise strongly on the next bet and when the next substitution is made stand pat, you are bluffing. As he follows you he will have to decide whether to play the 8 out to the end or trade in an effort to improve. Whether he stands pat or trades, you will trade your hole card on the final (third) substitution. Your prospect of bluffing him out of the pot is slim in a limit-stakes game, but it is not hard to bluff him into giving up his 8 in an attempt to improve. There are many examples of this kind of play in the substitution games. If you were sitting in back of the 8, you might get him to break it without giving up that second draw.

Some bluffing situations have a similarity to those of plain poker, where you are trying to force a player out of a pot. Such a situation was described earlier in pass the garbage. They tend to apply in games where an early decision to stay creates a large financial commitment for several rounds of betting, compared with the amount already invested. For bluffs of this type there is an old poker ditty that goes like this: Never bluff a winner. The other side of the coin is this: Losers never bluff. In part, these bits of wisdom are correct. The logic is too obvious to warrant detailed discussion. The heavy loser is ordinarily running scared, and he is intent upon avoiding a disastrous night. He doesn't try to bluff and on the other hand is an easy target for a bluff. The reverse psychology applies for the heavy winner. But there are exceptions and you must "know your man." The exceptions are the loser who runs amuck trying to recover and the winner who is intent on remaining a winner and becomes oh, so conservative.

All's fair in love and war

If the author of the above line had been a poker addict he would surely have modified the statement to "All's fair in love, poker and war." Poker is a game that involves cards, money and people. The people are in command of themselves as well as their cards and their money. They use all three to create a posture. There is a broad over-all posture and there is the posture on a particular hand. Each individual pot is a separate battle. You do anything, say anything within the rules and accepted conventions of your game to win the battle and to win the war. In most poker games it is acceptable to say whatever you choose about the cards on the table or to comment or needle a particular player. You are permitted to wince when you have pulled a 6 for a perfect low. You are permitted to hold your cards as though prepared to fold and comment, "My little pair of 6s will win the middle but not the high or low." Then when it comes your turn, raise the limit. You can also tell the truth, of course.

In most circles it is not cricket to comment on affairs not pertinent to the poker game in an effort to rile one of the players. You can criticize a man's poker ability but not his sex activity. You can comment on his stupidity in breaking aces in the previous hand but you cannot comment about his business, his politics, his wife, his children or his house. These are the normal conventions at poker. Of course, you cannot cheat. When a hand is completed and a strong low player who was not called tosses in his cards, you may not retrieve them to see if he really had it. Within these conventions you are free to act as you wish, provided you do not unduly delay the game or otherwise upset the physical aspects of the proceedings.

Academy awards here

Poker is a game where good acting pays off and poor acting pays off negatively. The word "acting" here applies generally and includes your conversation as well. Some players keep up a constant line of chatter that means nothing at all. They fiddle with a pipe, always have a drink at their elbows and chatter away. Others play a quiet game. The tricky player talks some and gestures a little, and tucked into this are little tidbits that influence the course of the proceedings. We had an example earlier ("Know your man") when Freddie was prepared to raise on K, Q, 8 up in seven-card stud. You knew it because he was fingering his chips the way he always does when he is going to raise. You said something about the missing 6s and Freddie paused. That one required good timing. It is amazing how often this sort of commentary works. The most obvious ruses will work against the inept player and sometimes against others. The high man bets on A♡, K♡, 3♡, 4♣ after the seventh card. You are second and would just as soon there was no raising. As you toss in your chips—"That's a mighty powerful two-way hand, buddy boy." Reverse it to a situation where you want some raising. You have a full house in seven stud after the sixth card and are high. You bet and, looking around, say, "Who has a low around here?" Either a player with a decent low or someone without a real low may raise. Then you can reraise. It doesn't work all the time, of course, but it works often enough.

Let's turn it around and consider your reaction to the conversation and posture of the others. It is preferable to pay no attention at all to the conversation and manner of the strong player. The chances are he'll outsmart you if you try. It is easier to ignore him. There will be times when you will be on the borderline. Let his message sink in, then think it over. Sometimes his message will help you. Usually it won't. When you have a flush or low decision to make in substitution and he is playing low, he will of course want you to go for the flush and this may be your best play. You will know how many hearts remain. If the message you get is "your low prospects are lousy," don't believe him. Check them yourself.

Watch each player. Do any of them have giveaway signs? The very best player sometimes does. It will be only in rare situations or else he would be a loser. You capitalize most in this department against the poor player.

17

Playing
with the Girls

Poker has always been a man's game. From the frontier days of the nineteenth century and in the front half of this century, men have been the poker players. To millions of Americans it is a vulgar business consigned to the sawdust-covered floors of a saloon in a dusty western town. This is the Hollywood or TV version of poker. It is fictional and romantic in a sense. In earlier pages we discussed the elements of a romanticized situation. This was the hand where Dundee folded four queens because Straights Fowler had raised just the right number of times—let us say five raises. Fowler held four kings, just as the fifth raise indicated. The chance of your holding four of a kind in draw poker and losing to a higher four of a kind is of the order of one in a million, which is just one step removed from saying that it can't happen. The good guy pulls a straight flush to win a pot that includes the mortgage on his future father-in-law's ranch. How thrilling!

Our society is changing rapidly. The past twenty years have seen greater change than in any similar preceding period. Year after year our national production increases. Not so long ago

the normal work week was six days and nine hours each day
—54 hours a week. The movement of population for perhaps a
century has been from the farms to the city. This trend has been
intensified in recent years, as it takes fewer and fewer workers
to produce the food needed to stock our supermarkets. But now
we see another trend—the movement from the city to the suburbs. This is the consequence of a shorter work week and improved transportation facilities. With further scientific and
engineering discoveries, the work week will be further shortened
and the working years of a man's life will also be reduced. And
on top of that the life span is constantly lengthened. We will
soon be retiring at sixty with the expectation of living to eighty.
(The insurance companies just love it.)

It adds up to more leisure. As a nation we seem to be using a
good-sized chunk of our increased productivity to buy more
leisure. It makes good sense in general, if we set aside periods of
national emergency when special needs must be met. You play
till twenty, work till sixty, and play till eighty. And you can expect a lot less work in that middle period.

The rapid increase in leisure time has brought about striking
changes in living habits and living standards. The do-it-your-
self craze is one example of this change. Along with it has come
a greater interest in games of all kinds. The history of bridge is
an example. Invented in its present form in the 1920s, bridge
has attracted an increasing number of players each year. It is an
excellent card game that brings out the best in people. Its popu-
larity has been aided by the work of two master publicists,
great players and teachers and distinguished personalities. Ely
Culbertson in the 1930s and Charles H. Goren in the postwar
years have made bridge a household game. There are today over
40,000,000 Americans playing bridge, according to the estimates
of bridge authorities. Most daily newspapers carry a column
by one or another of a number of bridge authorities—Goren,
Jacoby, Scheinwold, Blackwood, Schenken, and others. Walk
into a bookstore anywhere in the U.S.A. and count the bridge
books. You will find a dozen in the tiniest little store and per-

haps two dozen different titles in the large stores in New York or Los Angeles. The names of members of the bridge fraternity are nationally famous. Everyone knows of Goren, Jacoby, Roth, Stone, Crawford, *et al.* The bridge life of America is organized, and the daily results of three annual national tournaments, which last about eight days each, are reported in many daily newspapers. There is a monthly magazine, *The Bridge World,* which reports the results of these and other tournaments in great detail and with great care. The magazine reports other bridge events, contains humorous articles and serious, scholarly, technical articles. The magazine was originated by Ely Culbertson and is now published by Al Moyse, Jr.

Consider the postwar boom in bowling. This form of amusement, also a skill game, is even better organized then bridge and possibly more widely played. The investment in bowling alleys in the past ten years has been staggering. Each year the new establishments are bigger, more attractive, and provide better services in one way or another. They include comfortable restaurants. Facilities for parties of all types and even baby-sitting services are available. Turn to the television pages of your local newspaper. There are four or five bowling programs each week.

Return to those bookstores in search of a poker book. There may well be none. If it is a well-stocked, big-city bookstore you may find as many as four titles muddled among the many chess and bridge books. If you find books by Jacoby, Yardley, Steig and Moss (a soft cover), you're looking at practically the entire output of poker books in the last twenty years! There is a little more—a chapter here or there in a book on cards generally; the paperback Maverick book and maybe one or two pieces I have missed.

How many poker players are there in the United States? My guess is 20,000,000, a pretty staggering number when you realize that there is no literature and no organized society like the American Contract Bridge League. Who are the authorities in poker? Only the name of Oswald Jacoby seems to come to mind. For the most part poker is frowned upon as a game for ruffians.

It is not acceptable in polite circles. If a man is an outstanding bridge player, or bowler, he brings home shiny trophies that are proudly put on display. When he brings home that poker cabbage you mustn't whisper it to a soul.

Is there an explanation for this state of affairs? I say it is because the ladies have been excluded by every imaginable device from playing poker. For those who consider poker as man's private domain, as man's sole retreat, as the final outpost of virility, I'll concede. Of all others I ask this: Why not a men's game on Friday as in the past and a coed game on Saturday? It may be a drag for a few months, but you'll be pleasantly surprised after a while. It can be loads of fun even if it is played for pennies.

But what games? I have another theory on that score and this I'll argue with anyone and forever. Try to teach the ladies five-card stud, jacks, or draw with guts to open played for pennies and they'll be discussing recipes and drapes and children in no time at all. It must be the high-low games. Give them a couple of months and, as the psychologists put it, you'll find a new community of interest. As you clean the ash trays and rearrange the furniture, she'll be asking what your down card was on the hand where Paul bet four cents and she raised and you reraised. You'll discover that she doesn't mind your Friday-night game nearly so much as she used to (don't expect perfection). You'll have to post-mortem the "big" game on Saturday mornings as she serves your bacon and eggs over light. You may even discover a refreshing respect when she observes at first hand how good you really are.

Here are a couple of pointers on running such a game. A couple must always be separated. They may not sit side by side. This is recommended in any circumstances but especially if you include push as one of your games. You'll never be able to explain that it would have been cheating to pass the jack that she coveted.

Only a player who has dropped and hasn't looked at anyone else's cards is allowed to help one of the ladies. This is vital in the early months. When you fold, wait until help is needed; don't lean over and look at your neighbor's cards. Instead, be available to help. It speeds up the game and can be the difference between getting beyond those early trying months and a flop. They will be difficult months and will require loads of patience.

Most important of all, each person must play for himself. Family play can ruin a game that would otherwise offer years of pleasure and satisfaction. You come to this three-man (man now is generalized to mean either sex) ending in seven-card stud:

	Down			*Up*			
Mr. A				K♠	J♣	8♡	8◇
Mr. B				Q♡	8♠	5♠	2♣
Mrs. A	3♠	4♣	9◇	7♠	10♡	9♡	9♣

Mr. A calls first and announces high. B calls low. If Mrs. A declares low on 10 rather than high on the three 9s, it is a family call. Here is another example: Mrs. B has a lock for low in three-card substitution and there are three high players, including Mr. B. In these circumstances the three high players, unless one of them is exceptionally strong, are well advised to check and merely call Mrs. B's bet. This is a normal and common situation where three players are fighting it out for the high against one low player. If Mr. B starts raising on high cards that don't call for any raises, it is a family play.

In short, each person should play his own hand and compete with his spouse just as he would with any other player. A little family rivalry is all to the good. We have one in our game, and it is worth an admission fee. They needle each other mercilessly when a bad call or other error is made.

I can't remember precisely how our coed game got under way. It started accidently about three years ago. In the beginning each of the girls had a list which showed the sequence of hands. It showed the perfect 6, 4, 3, 2, A; 6, 5, 3, 2, A was next; it went up to the straight flush and finally to five of a kind, which beats a straight flush in wild-card games. That first night was chaos. Three of the girls knew nothing of poker and the fourth knew just a bit more. You should see them now. The lists have long been forgotten. Some of them play a pretty sound game; others not so good. They are not the strongest by any means, but they all can outplay Freddie. The stakes are small so that no one gets hurt badly—two cents and four cents—and everyone plays a loose, carefree game. Discussion of recipes and children is forbidden. Some mighty odd things occur.

You are in the midst of a hotly contested hand of twin beds. It is 10:45. The phone rings. Peggy is calling her mother, but Al is closer and takes the phone. Peggy reports that big brother Bruce, who was to be back from a party at 10:30, is not home. Al tells Peggy to go to bed but to leave a note for Bruce to call. He puts the phone back in its cradle, but it rings again. Charlotte reporting that she is home from her date. Phone rings again. Jerry reporting that he is home. The phone is replaced in its cradle and it rings once more. Amy is home from the high-school basketball game. You hang up the phone. Can it ring again? It does. Al reaches for the phone and says, "Bruce, you're late; go right to bed." A pause. "Never mind how I knew it was you; go to bed this minute."

He knew because there were no teen-agers left. They completed the hand of twin beds.

The game is three-card substitution. The stakes are two and four cents; the ante is two cents; three raises per round; no sandbagging. Let's play the hand with Al. After the regular five cards were dealt, the layout was as diagramed below. The first substitution is shown also.

	Down		Up			Draw
Marge		A♣	2◊	6◊	Q♠	5◊
Paul		3♠	4♡	2♣	J♡	A♡
Carol		9◊	K♣	6♡	K♠	J♣
Fred		7♡	5♣	10♡	4♠	10◊
Al	5♡	6♠	8◊	Q♡	7♣	9♣

The underlined cards were pitched and replaced by the cards shown to the right. Al was pleased with this turn of events. Only Carol could beat his straight by pulling a full house—he thought. He had seen the girls make some mighty weird plays, but couldn't anticipate this one. Carol bet four cents and both Al and Paul raised strongly. Carol killed it, making a total of fourteen cents. When the second trade started, Marge was in a sweat. It appeared as though she had a high diamond in the hole rather than a low card. She had been playing a few months. She studied Paul's cards and finally ditched the ace of clubs, going for the flush, but failed. Paul didn't have his low. He tossed his hole card: "I'll take a secret one." There was another round of betting and on the third substitution Marge drew the jack of diamonds. Fred won the low with a 7, as Paul never made it. Marge had her flush, but Al was stunned when she turned not a high diamond but the 4 of diamonds. She had broken a 6, 5, 4 low to go for the flush, when only the case 6 as Paul's down card could possibly beat her for low. The 2, 4, 5, 6 all in diamonds was more than Marge could resist. She just had to go for the straight flush and she was sort of displeased that she had made only an ordinary flush.

Al stared at her cards in bewilderment. "Do you like the high half better than the low half of the pot?"

"That's a real good funny," Marge replied.

In the early days whenever a new game was played something odd occurred. Six-card pass the garbage is a strange game. The hands can run strong or very poor. In seven-card pass the garbage the hands are usually solid, but it cannot be played with eight. In six-card garbage four players stayed for the rolling, and after the third card, this was the layout.

Bill	7♡	4♡	8♡
Marie	6◇	5♠	2◇
Eleanor	4♣	A♣	6♣
Fred	K◇	J♣	Q♣

The betting was tame enough, but Marie dropped out. Another card was turned.

Bill	7♡	4♡	8♡	K♡
Eleanor	4♣	A♣	6♣	10♣
Fred	K◇	J♣	Q♣	9♡

When these cards were turned Marie said, "Boy, am I glad I dropped. I was really whipped for high." Al, who was annoyed anyway because he had folded an 8 low, responded to his wife's comment: "Yes, your little straight was the fourth highest, which was also the lowest. After all you invested you might have spent four cents to see another card. Besides you should have folded immediately with that hand." Startled, she stared at the table and it became clear that they were all high players with two flushes and a high straight. No legitimate low was in the game. Bill won the high with an A, K flush, and Fred took the low half on a high straight.

Fred had been betting and raising, but he finished with an in-between hand when the final down card in seven-card high-low was dealt.

	Down			*Up*			
Marge				A◇	4♡	4♠	2♡
Fred	8♣	3◇	10♡	2♣	8♡	A♠	3♠
Al				J◇	7◇	A♡	6♡
Bill				5♠	8◇	6♣	5♣

Al had also been raising throughout. Fred concluded that they were all in the low department and that he would continue a show of strength and call high on his little two pair. This was a pretty good plan. On the final round of betting Bill also tossed in a raise. When the betting ended, Fred continued the display and, with an air of confidence, called high. But it wasn't his call. After the dust had settled on this bit of confusion, Bill, the last raiser, announced high and Marge, without any thought, also called high. Fred sheepishly studied his cards. "Don't think I can win the high any more, so I'll have to call low."

Al stared at his cards in stony silence. He called low, adding, "I wish you did have to declare first. I have a jack for low."

Fred won the low with a 10. Marge got half the pot with three 4s, which beat kings over 5s.

Al had a bad run one evening. He hadn't won a pot all night, but he had played cautiously and was down only $1.62. A hand of twin beds, use one on either side, was dealt. This is a confusing game in the sense that there are so many combinations possible. There are 25 possible two-card combinations of the center cards. When the final two center cards were turned Al found that he had four aces. A big pot would put him near even. As the betting proceeded it was clearly going to be a big one. Without much concern Al raised four cents at each opportunity. Carol and Eleanor also raised freely. When the last roll was made Al stared at Carol's cards.

Center Cards

Q♣   J♦
A♦   8♣
4♥   10♠
K♠   2♣
K♦   A♥

	Down	Up			
Al	A♣	7♥	9♦	A♠	5♣
Carol		Q♦	2♥	9♣	3♥
Eleanor		10♥	K♣	6♠	4♠

Eleanor had a perfect, this was clear. She never raised until she had a winner, but Carol could have a straight flush if her final card was the 5♥, for the A♥ and 4♥ could be used and she had already rolled the 2♥ and 3♥. She could also have a perfect low. Fred and Marge were also in, but were merely sweetening the pot. The final bet was made.

Al winced when Carol announced high. Imagine losing in this game with four aces. As there were several 16-cent rounds of betting, he was down almost three bucks. He didn't win a pot the balance of that evening.

Perhaps one should not quarrel with success, but I do not recommend Marge's play on this hand. Al drew a pair of open kings in seven-card high-low on the fourth card and bet the limit. On the fifth card he bet, Bill raised, Al raised and Bill raised. By the time the raising was all over, only Marge remained in the pot with the two fellows. Bill showed three low cards. On the sixth card Al failed to improve and Bill drew another low card. The bet again reached 16 cents. After the final down card was dealt this was the layout:

	Down			*Up*			
Marge				8♢	10♣	4♢	7♠
Al	Q♠	10♡	4♣	K♡	K♢	6♡	J♡
Bill				A♢	5♣	8♠	6♠

The betting again reached 16 cents on three raises, and Bill declared first. He announced low and Al called high. Al had gone into the final round with a pair of kings, a four flush, and a bobtail draw to a straight. He had pulled the 4♣, which didn't help at all. He bet strongly on the final round to maintain the show of strength. Bill had also bet strongly without any faltering.

Marge was in a quandary. She showed her hand to Fred, who shrugged his shoulders. Finally she squeaked, "I don't know which way to go. I guess I'm beat either way, so I'll call both ways." Al looked at Bill helplessly, but found Bill in a state of shock. Marge had muddled her cards into the discards, thinking she didn't have a chance, but when order was restored the hands were these:

Marge	8	3	7	8	10	4	7
Al	Q	10	4	K	K	6	J
Bill	J	6	Q	A	5	8	6

Marge had two small pair for high and a 10 low. In spite of their powerful-looking hands, Bill and Al didn't have much. Bill had a jack for low. His sixth card had paired him and his seventh was a picture. Al had only the kings he started with, so Marge won it both ways.

Marge had made a poor percentage play in calling both ways. You occasionally face this situation. You have played to the end and are weak both ways. It is foolhardy to call both ways. Ordinarily there will be some indication that one of the opponents is not strong, or not so strong as he wants to appear. Or you may know one of the players is an end-game thief. If they both bet heavily and there is no clue or giveaway that one of them is phony, you simply have to guess. The prospect of winning both ways in a situation comparable to the one just described is so remote that it should never be attempted. It is one step removed from conceding the pot, and you should never do that.

Here is a bizarre ending which illustrates that you must always be alert and understand the proceedings. We'll watch Al play it. He had stayed in a hand of three-card sub, playing for the high, and wasn't too happy about his prospects. One trade had already been made, and this was the layout:

	Down		Up		
Fred		9	A	5	5
Eleanor		7	4	8	4
Paul		J	J	10	3
Al	Q	6	3	Q	10

It looked as though Eleanor would pitch the 4 to develop a low, and she didn't seem to have much competition. Paul was clearly playing high. Fred might toss either the 5 or the 9. If he held a low hole card he might become a low contender. The second trade cost eight cents. Freddie stayed for the bet. When it came time to trade, Fred ditched the 9. He received a 5 for three of a kind. Now Eleanor went into a huddle. Al knew that she was holding at least two pair and was debating whether to break them for low or compete against Fred for high. Two small pair are frequently a nuisance in this game. She went for the full house and didn't make it.

Paul broke for low. He pitched a jack. He pulled a jack! That's how the cookie crumbles.

Al now tossed his hole card and pulled a deuce. After a round of betting, the final 12-cent trade commenced with this layout:

	Down		*Up*		
Fred		A	5	5	5
Eleanor		4	8	4	K
Paul		J	10	3	J
Al	2	6	3	Q	10

Fred pulled a hole card. Eleanor got a 9 in place of her king. Paul tossed the jack. He shuddered when another 3 came off the top of the deck. Al didn't even have to spend 12 cents to buy. He held a lock with a queen low!

Then there was the night the police were roaming the neighborhood. After some checking around we discovered that they were searching in the woods, an undeveloped tract, for some thieves. Marge turned pale. Her three youngsters were home alone and she was on her way. She and Bill owned the house that bordered the undeveloped tract. The ladies were all sympathetic. In the middle of a hand of twin beds, all the players picked up their chips, their rolled cards, their closed cards, the center cards, the chips in the pot, and the coffee pot, and moved a block up the hill. They arrived to find the children sound asleep. The seating arrangement, center cards and rolled cards were restored as before. Coffee was poured and the game resumed.

I am indebted to Peter Schwed of Simon and Schuster for the following suggestion. It seems most appropriate for social circumstances where it is a mixed game or where the players are at different income levels, or have inflated notions of their ability, or for a myriad of other reasons. Each player is permitted to select his own stakes. There might be three or four levels from which a choice is permitted. For example, the ladies might select 2, 4, and 6 cents. Another permissible range might be 5, 10 and 15. The plunger might play 10, 20 and 30, and 20, 40 and 60 cents may be also permitted. Each player selects the level that particularly suits his fancy for the evening. An impecunious novelist would surely be a 2, 4 and 6 man. The hot-shot account executive might be expected to play for higher stakes but for a lark might also select 2, 4 and 6. He could then bet and raise with abandon, placing the big gamblers under severe pressure which would develop some unusual and striking end games.

Each person makes his choice of stakes in privacy, recording it on a slip of paper. The folded slips are passed to the host in exchange for a stack of chips. The slips are hidden for the evening. The betting is generalized as one chip, two chips or three chips. Of course everyone comments at one time or another on the stakes he is playing—lying at times, perhaps telling the truth. When the play is completed each slip is opened. It would be a riot to see the hot-shot player lose after he has chosen high stakes.

This form of variable stakes requires either a bank or a banker. If the big gamblers win and the penny players lose, the bank loses. In the reverse case the bank would gain. If one person chooses to bank the game, he is gambling that the low-stakes players will outplay the high-stakes players. One way to start such a game—which I am sure will provide many entertaining moments—is to have each couple chip in ten dollars. If the bank wins over a period of several months, it can then be used to finance an evening on the town. If it loses, the bank can be replenished by taxing the winners.

18

A Dialogue
with Al

You were invited to the poker game at Al's house. You decided to attend but only as an observer. Hours later when the others have left, you decide to stay behind. As you help Al empty the ash trays and rearrange the furniture, you ask a few questions.

You: Early in the game you won a pot on jacks over 8s in three-card sub. You raised on the two pair only for the final bet when you clearly had it won. The earlier rounds went begging for a raise. Bill won the low and he was needling you when you merely called. How come?

AL: I remember that one. It is a common problem and warrants careful study. It was a four-player ending. My two pair weren't live, if you recall. Both jacks and one 8 were dead. Before the first substitution Herb held a pair of kings, and it was clear that he didn't have two pair as the play progressed. But if you recall Herb's cards, they were very live. No kings had shown and one of his up cards was a 9 which was also live. His hole card must have been pretty good too, because on the second substitution he ditched a queen and only one other queen had shown. In short, while I had two pair and Herbie had only kings, he had an excellent chance of improving to beat me. I think he held a deuce down, because on the last substitution when Fred pulled a deuce Herb looked at it despairingly.

Furthermore, while Fred looked like a low player, his cards might have made a straight. He held 7, 5, 4 and an odd card up. I think he held a 3 or 6 in the hole and had a chance to beat me for high by pulling a straight. He pulled a deuce and lost to Bill's 7, 4, but Freddie never did show his down card.

When the substitutions started, I decided to play to minimize my losses rather than to go for a big pot. My chance of improving the two pair was so slim that I didn't want to invest in buying more cards, and my chance of ending up a loser was pretty strong. By not raising and not buying, I held my cost to 30 cents a round. Of course on the final round, when I had it made, I raised. While I didn't win a big pot, my loss would have been light if Herb improved or Fred made a straight. This play gave me the best gamble. Two pair losing can be a very expensive proposition in three-card sub when you pay for all the substitutions and there is a lot of raising.

You: That sounds familiar. I think I read something similar in a book not long ago. How about the hand of push when you dropped out on 7, 6, 3 up and a deuce down? That seemed like an awfully strange play on such good low cards. Do you remember the hand or did you misread the cards?

AL: No, I didn't misread the cards. Have you ever heard this little gem. There is a saying in baseball circles that the best trade a manager sometimes makes is the trade he chooses not to make. This has its counterpart in poker. The money you don't invest by dropping out of a pot before the betting gets steep is the equivalent of winning a small pot. I win a lot of small pots that way in hands I concede early in the play. It is much more glamorous to take your winnings out of the center of the table. And of course you have to win some of the pots, but protecting the chips right under your chin is plenty important too.

If you recall the hand, the player to my right had very similar cards to mine, so he surely wasn't going to pass me any low cards that would help. In addition, good old Freddie was in for high and Paul, sitting to his left, was a low player. That meant Paul was in a strong position, because he could easily be pushed low cards by Freddie. Paul is a clever player and I was pretty sure he would start betting heavy in that position, and, if you recall, he did. So I dropped with what seemed like a good hand. The hand cost me only 40 cents—10 cents for the ante, a 10-cent bet and a 20-cent bet. Why go for a big investment in this perilous situation? There are more pots to come.

You: I get the idea. I guess the same type of explanation applied to the twin-beds hand you dropped with 9s full just before the game broke up. There wasn't a pair showing in the center cards. The pot was won by kings full, and you would have lost plenty.

Al: You bet I would have lost plenty in the hand. There were a lot of high cards in the center and few low cards. The high competition was going to be tough in spite of the absence of a pair. I hate those draggy, middle-type hands like an 8 low or two pair in substitution or a small full house in regular twin beds. But there was another feature in that particular hand. When the next to last two center cards were turned, which were a king and a jack, Frankie boy became very quiet. He was fingering his chips as though ready to raise, but he changed his mind. I guess he was afraid of driving out some customers by raising too early, and he didn't want it to look as though one of those two cards had helped, so he held back. He did raise on the next card. Frank is a solid, conservative player. He bluffs on very rare occasions. Ordinarily when he raises, he's got it.

Poor Freddie got whipsawed on that pot, didn't he? It must have cost him close to five bucks to play 8s full. I folded 9s full. That happens all the time. I drop out and find Freddie playing a poorer hand than the one I dropped with.

You: Freddie got a real shellacking tonight, didn't he? But your comment about Frank reminds me of a pot where you raised and then dropped out. It was a pass-the-garbage hand and you went with queens and 10s. The three cards passed to you were low ones. You tried to bluff a full house and then folded.

AL: That was against Bill. I've been laying for him. Bill is good. He's getting too damn good. He's been folding some real good hands against me and I'm going to have to do something about it. He's been playing me as though he sees my cards. Maybe I've been telegraphing my hand or maybe I've become too conservative the last few months, but Bill has made a monkey out of me recently. You know there was a pot tonight when I think he folded a 6, 5 against me when I had a perfect in twin beds. I wish I had seen his card.

YOU: But what about the garbage hand?

AL: I figured I had to loosen him up—so I tried a bluff. Garbage is a good bluffing game on the high side when you can make a show of a high full house early in the betting.

YOU: I get it, but he played you right again. He stayed on a small full house.

AL: He sure did. But even though he played it right, I think it shook him a little and it didn't cost me much. Earlier, when I made a flush in substitution, he dropped; remember that one. You know, I thought I would never see the day when anyone would mark me as an overly conservative player. But I have a lot of respect for Bill, at poker or anything else. He hasn't been playing high-low very long—only a couple of years—but if he has been playing me for an "old man," there is probably something in it. I think this has been going on for only a little while, and so it will take only a couple of good shots to fix Bill. It may take a few evenings till the right spot comes along, but he'll remember it when it comes.

YOU: I didn't realize such personal situations developed.

AL: Brother, they sure do. Bill is actually a trickier player than I am. Of course some of those tricky deals don't come off and I don't believe in overdoing it. Bill may well overdo it.

YOU: I gathered from some of the guys that you have a reputation as a slick, unpredictable player.

AL: That's true. The best image you can have is to be reputed to be tricky. Then you can play conservatively, without paying out any advertising money, and get called on all your good hands. As I have pointed out, though, Bill seems to be on to me, and I'll have to do some advertising.

YOU: There was one thing I meant to ask you. I noticed one hand of seven-card where you already had a 6 low and made a big show out of squeezing the last card which you didn't need at all. Why the big act?

AL: I'll tell you one of my big secrets. I have a very bad habit that I have trouble shaking. When I need that seventh card badly I sometimes can't help placing it between my other two hole cards and squeezing. Sometimes I remember not to do it, but it's a very old habit from the days when I played draw and other high-only games and I slip sometimes. Consequently I try to cover for it occasionally by going through the same act when I don't need the last card at all. Herb also has the same habit. He is an old draw-poker man.

YOU: What about the seven-card hand where you held a flush and a low? I thought you were going to call both ways, but you merely called low. Frank had a full house, so it turned out right. But how did you know?

AL: I didn't know, of course. But early in that pot, Frank seemed real happy with his high cards. I know Frank. He doesn't play for high very often, but when he does, he's holding strong. He started with a 9 and pulled a 10, then a 9. Frank would fold at that point if he held only one pair, unless he held four to a straight. Most likely, though, he had started the hand with a pair and was now holding two pair or three of a kind. He picked up another 10 on the sixth card. So I figured my flush wasn't enough. I guess it comes down to my knowing Frank. When he plays with high cards at the beginning in seven-card high-low, he has a pair.

YOU: Tell me this: do you play the same way for pennies as you did tonight? And what about a bigger game—would you play the same way?

AL: In the penny game we play with our wives, I play a much

looser game. Of course, everyone else does too. I don't throw my money away, but it is normal to loosen up. Tonight's game was no cheap affair—I'm sure you'll agree to that—and I play it pretty tight. But in a really big game, a lot depends on the opponents. In general I play a little closer than tonight in a bigger game. For example, in a dollar-limit game, I would probably fold in push on 7, 9. In tonight's game I would play it if the 9 was up and I would get a crack at getting rid of the 9. You know, first position frequently works out very well in push because you always get two shots at fresh cards. You don't get the other guy's garbage.

Getting back to your question: I do play a little more conservatively on the first bet in a big game compared with the 10, 20, 30 game. From then on I play about the same. In a big game, I probably pay more attention to how my luck has been running than in a smaller game. I drop in situations I might play at 10, 20, 30 because I "feel" it's not right for me.

You: But I thought you don't believe in luck. I've heard you make nasty comments about it many times.

AL: Certainly the cards you get over a long run will be about equal in quality with those of any other player's. The quality of the cards you will get on the next hand is independent of the cards you received on previous hands—yet they do seem to come in streaks sometimes. More importantly, though, I used the word "luck" earlier to mean the way things seem to be breaking for me independently of the cards. I don't expect to get a 6 low in stud often, but when I do I'm in good luck if I have a strong high player with me. I'm in bad luck if there is no one else raising and I can't build a big pot. I'm in bad luck when I'm asleep at the table and miss one of Fred's giveaways. For this sort of thing I sometimes don't feel right and I miss things. I forget a folded card or something like that. Maybe luck isn't the right word. Maybe I should say on nights when I think I'm playing poorly I play much more conservatively in a high-stakes game. You would be surprised how your physical and psychological condition is important in poker. The worst losing streak I ever had in poker came at a time when I blew a few thousand dollars in a business venture. I was preoccupied with the business and I just wasn't sharp at the poker table.

You: Why play under such conditions?

Al: Well, of course, that is the answer. It is probably wise to stay away from a big-stakes game when you're not feeling well or under some strain because of business problems. But I never seem to think of refusing. What's more, I just can't imagine telling the guys that I wasn't going to play poker because I screwed up the Anderson account at work. Besides, I like to play poker, and one rarely can admit, even to himself, that he is under pressure. After I have played a few hands and find that I'm off beat, I tighten up.

You: I've heard some players say that you should never bet on the come. Yet it is done all the time.

Al: Listen, there is no such thing as never or always in poker. If the guy knows what he is talking about, he's using the word in a generalized sense to mean it isn't a good percentage play in many situations. "Never bet on the come" mainly applies to high-only games, and ordinarily it is pretty good advice. In the high-low games, the situations are much too complicated to develop clichés of this kind. I sometimes raise in seven-card when I have a four flush in the first four cards, and I sometimes do the same when I have two of the same suit up and the hole cards don't match. Of course, in the latter situation, I do it only when I have some other strong situation to develop. I don't do it simply to bluff a flush.

You: When you played a hand of murder early in the evening you stood pat for the first trade with an ace down, 3 up. Why did you give up a draw when you get only three chances of making the hand? You pitched the ace on the second substitution.

Al: If you remember the hand, Herb raised on a 4 up and I raised and he raised. He could have a 2, 3, or 4 down to explain his action. If he had the pair of 4s, I had to play for low, and if he had the 2 or 3, I should go for high. As it might have been fatal for me to guess at that point, I felt it was best to give up a trade to get more information. On the next round one of the others pulled a deuce up, and Herb bet just as strongly against my 3 up and the 2 up, even though I raised against him. I concluded that he held a pair of 4s and I went for low. If you recall, I was right, as I ended up winning half the pot on 5, 3.

You: I noticed that you folded a 7, 5 in twin beds use one on each side. I thought 7 was a good low in that game. After all, a guy needs three good cards in his hand to make any low at all, so a 7 is pretty good.

AL: A 6 is good and a deep 7 will sometimes win in use on each side, but in the pot you are referring to there were a lot of low cards in the center—three in each colum. As a consequence *everyone* with three low cards in his hand would have a low. I didn't have much of a chance. Remember what I said about the equivalent of winning a small pot by staying out of big pots? This was one of those hands.

You: But a 7, 5 won it.

AL: Yes, a 7, 5, 3, 2, A. That's a pretty deep 7 low.

You: You sure seem proud of that phrase "win a small pot by staying out of expensive situations with draggy hands."

AL: You bet I'm proud of it. The most common and most expensive error made by poor players is being in pots they should be watching. All the other fancy stuff about bluffing and high strategy and card reading is unimportant compared with chasing on medium hands. They can't possibly pay off in the long run. You must have patience to play poker and be willing to wait for playable cards—not a cinch, just cards that give you a good gamble. I'm no phrasemaker, but I'm even prouder of this one: "When in doubt, drop out."

Appendixes

Appendix A

Quiz

1. Seven-card stud, high-low

	Down	Up	
A		K♠ 9♣	9♦
B		8♣ 4♠	A♠
C		7♡ 2♡	10♠
D		5♦ 5♣	Q♦
You			

There was a 10-cent ante. A 10-cent bet on the first round caused two players to fold the J♦ and 9♠. All others called. A 20-cent bet was called all around on the second up card, and A bet 30 cents, which was called by B, C and D on the third up card.

What is your action on each of the following?

	Down		Up		
(1)	6♠	6♡	A♦	2♦	5♠
(2)	6♠	6♡	A♦	J♠	10♣
(3)	6♠	J♠	8♡	8♦	10♣
(4)	6♠	J♠	8♡	8♦	7♣
(5)	7♣	J♠	6♠	A♦	2♦
(6)	Q♡	8♡	10♣	7♣	8♦

(7) What is your action on the same set of hands in the following circumstances: A bets 30, B raises to 60, C calls, and D raises to 90.

(8) B is a very conservative and sound player. What kind of a holding would his raise suggest if you are holding 6♠, A♢, 2♡ up?

2. Three-card substitution

	Down		Up	
A	6♡	Q♢	Q♡	10♣
B	4♠	6♣	J♡	5♠
C	9♠	A♣	10♠	9♡
You				

The conditions are as usual. Cards folded earlier were K♠, J♢, 8♣. The bets were: 10 cents first round; 20 cents second round; 30 cents third round. On this round A bets 30 cents, B and C call. You are the dealer. What do you do with each of the following?

	Down		Up		
(1)	2♠	3♣	K♡	7♠	A♢
(2)	2♠	3♣	K♡	8♢	A♢
(3)	J♣	J♠	K♡	5♣	6♢
(4)	8♢	3♣	K♡	A♢	2♠
(5)	2♣	3♣	K♡	A♢	2♠

(6) C is the author of this bit of literature. What is my probable hole card with 9, A, 10, 9 showing and the circumstances described above?

(7) Assume that the first substitution went as shown, with the underlined card discarded and the card at the right received as the replacement.

	Down			Up		
A		6♡	Q♠	Q♢	10♣	K♣
B		4♠	6♣	J♡	5♠	5♡
C		9♠	A♣	10♠	9♡	4♡
You	2♣	3♣	K♡	A♢	2♠	7♢

A bets 30. B and C call. What do you do?

(8) Suppose you raised and A reraised. In the midst of this, A turned over a glass of water. As he was drying his cards, he dropped the hole card on the floor and you saw it. It was the K♠. Who is A?

3. Twin beds (regular style)

Center	Cards
7♡	Q♢
6♠	9♣
5♣	J♢
4♢	10♣
K♣	10♢

The ante was a dime, and the first four rounds of betting were 10 cents, 20 cents, 20 cents and 20 cents, with no raising; now the bet is 30 cents. What is your action on each of the following hands in second position?

(1)	A♠	3♣	8♢	6♢	Q♣
(2)	A♠	2♣	8♢	6♢	Q♣
(3)	10♠	6♢	6♡	4♣	A♠
(4)	A♠	A♢	A♣	2♢	3♣
(5)	A♠	2♢	3♣	8♣	K♠
(6)	10♠	J♣	K♠	A♢	7♡

(7) How should Hand 4 be rolled as your best effort to conceal your strength in preparation for a two-way call with four others calling the fifth bet?

(8) Which of the following hands would you rather hold before any of the center cards are turned?

(a)   K♠ K♡ Q♠ Q♣ 6♡
(b)   9♠ 9♣ 9◇ A♣ 10♡

Answers

1. Seven-card stud, high-low

(1) Raise. You have an excellent low working and a good prospect on the high side with two 6s and two aces still live. You might even take both ends of it. Build as big a pot as you can.

(2) Call. You won't get rich playing these, but in last position you may as well see another card.

(3) Fold.

(4) Fold. Don't let the straight or possible low drag you into this pot. You have lost 40 cents. If you call this bet you may be "lucky" and make an 8, 7 low. You'll then have the divine pleasure of holding a second-best hand.

(5) Raise. Your low prospects are excellent.

(6) Your answer to this one should have been, "Does this idiot author think I would have played these cards?"

(7) With the two raises ahead of you, fold 3, 4 and 6 as before. Fold 2 also, even if Mr. D is a very tricky player and might be on a swindle of some kind. 1 and 5 are a matter of style. Call or raise is optional. If you expect B to make it $1.20, let him be the tough guy.

(8) B's hole cards might be two low spades, a low card and an ace, or any two low cards making an 8 low which is also live for improving to a better low or a straight or both.

2. Three-card substitution

(1) Call or raise is acceptable.

(2) Call. Only one low competitor.

(3) Fold. As the jacks are dead, your best probable improvement is to pull a king in one of the substitutions. See the answer to 6 for more on this problem.

(4) Raise. Start the pressure on B. You may wind up winning with an 8. You may even drive B into a high play if his hand is "right." Or you may drive him out. As you are sitting behind him, you have a significant advantage on this type of hand. You will see the result of his substitutions. (Note that 2 and 4 are the same holding with the down card changed.)

(5) Raise. Make him squirm.

(6) Probably an ace; maybe a 9. No other card makes sense at this point. With any other card the hand should certainly have folded by now.

(7) Raise; continue the ploy.

(8) Freddie, of course. And he isn't bluffing three queens. He really thinks his two pair is a winner.

3. Twin beds (regular style)

(1) Fold. This low won't win it. The low cards are much too live to hope that no other player will have A, 2.

(2) A lot closer. You will lose to A, 2, 3 in a hand; tie A, 2; beat A, 3. When you tie or win, it won't be much of a pot. When you lose it will cost, as the perfect will raise and raise. Fold.

(3) Fold. Tens full of 6s is not playable in this situation.

(4) Call. A raise here would be catastrophic. You must hold as many players as possible. A raise in second position might drive out all the borderline hands. And this layout figures to have two or three borderline hands. By holding off one round (or perhaps two) you may have them so deeply committed

that they will play all the way even after you start raising. This holding should take both ends of the pot.

(5) Call. Same logic as 4. Raise in a *very* loose game.

(6) Call now, but you shouldn't have played this to start.

(7) 3, then A, then A; after that it depends on what shows and how the betting has gone, but ordinarily the 2 should be turned next. Among the many unknowns and variables that can exist, this fact is clear: only one opponent can be playing low—the man holding the remaining A. Showing the perfect may cause him to drop. The remaining contestants are high players, and showing the aces full at this fourth roll will cause more than one player to drop.

(8) The chances are almost two out of three that you will make the big full house or four of a kind when the ten center cards are turned with the (a) hand. The chances are near 100 per cent that you will make 9s full or better on (b). But the (a) hand is better.

The features to be considered are:

The number of times full house or better makes.

The number of times the full house or better will win.

The size of pot when it wins.

The cost when it loses.

Hand (a) comes off much better. It is hurt comparatively only when the full house makes, but loses the hand. It wins bigger pots when the full house is made because it is strong enough to raise at every opportunity. Hand (a) folds early for a small loss when the full house doesn't come in. Hand (b) wins somewhat more often (65 per cent compared to 55 per cent), but it wins smaller pots. Furthermore, its losses tend to be large, as 9s full will usually play to the bitter end unless particularly strong high cards show in the common center cards.

Appendix B

A Problem in Figuring the Odds

In Chapter 2 we noted an incorrect solution of a very simple five-card-stud poker problem. This was a problem of determining the odds you receive in a particular situation. Our explanation in the text was in sufficient detail to explain the error. A more exacting solution is given here.

The problem:

	Down		Up	
You	10♠	6♠	4♠	8♠
Opponent	?	J◇	K♡	K♣

Eleven chips are already in the pot and opponent bets two chips (the limit). There are 36 unexposed cards of which six are spades, as opponents folding earlier in the hand turned three spades. The chance is one out of six that you will pull a spade.

Is it correct for you to call for two chips and see the final card?

We shall study the problem over a set of six hands, as this simplifies the computations. (See pages 212 and 213.)

The result shows that it is the correct play to try for the flush under the conditions given. The odds are about 1.35 to 1 in your favor; that is, for every $1.00 you put in you should get back $1.35 if this situation were repeated thousands of times. Note all the assumptions required in solving a very simple problem. Can you imagine all the assumptions and branches that would follow from a complex seven-card-stud high-low problem? Merely recording the results of computations would take many pages, and the computations would require weeks.

Event	Frequency of occurrence in a set of six hands	Chips lost that hand	over set	Chips won that hand	over set	Remarks
Don't get spade:	5	2	10.0000			Five times out of six you should fail to make the flush. You do not call the final bet in these five cases.
Get spade (opponent checks)	1					
Opponent does not get K or J	.89					Assume 28/36 (or .89) that he will not pull K or J.
Calls your final bet of 2 chips:	1 × .89 × .5 = .445			15	6.6750	Assume that he doesn't call your bet half the time (.5).
Does not call your final bet:	1 × .89 × .5 = .445			13	5.7850	
Opponent gets K or J	.11					4/36 is .11 that he does get K or J. Assume he has a K or J in the hole one out of five times (.20); that he will check, you will bet, he will raise, and you will always call his raise.
Has full house:	1 × .11 × .20 = .022	6	.1320			

Event	Frequency of occurrence in a set of six hands	Chips lost		Chips won		Remarks
		that hand	over set	that hand	over set	
Does not have full house	.80					4/5 is .80 that he does not have K or J as down card.
Tries to bluff:	$1 \times .11 \times .80 \times .10 = .0088$			17	.1496	Assume he tries to bluff once in ten (.10) and that you always call as you did when he had the full house.
Does not try to bluff						
Calls your final bet:	$1 \times .11 \times .8 \times .9 \times .5 = .0396$			15	.5940	Assume he calls your bet half the time as above.
Does not call your bet:	$1 \times .11 \times .8 \times .9 \times .5 = .0396$			13	.5148	
TOTALS	6.000		10.1320		13.7184	

Note: The final probabilities apply in a set of six hands, and the values shown in the "over set" columns are the amounts in the "that hand" column times the final values in the "frequency" column.

Appendix C: Sequence of Hands

Part 1—High hands

FIVE OF A KIND: This occurs only in wild-card games. Where two
hands with five of a kind compete, the higher denomination
or higher rank wins. Thus, five aces beats five kings and so on.

ROYAL FLUSH: The five highest cards of a suit, such as 10◇, J◇,
Q◇, K◇, A◇ (the highest straight flush).

STRAIGHT FLUSH: Five cards in the same suit and in sequence,
such as 9♣, 8♣, 7♣, 6♣, 5♣. Where two straight flushes compete, the winner is the hand with the higher top card in the
straight flush. Thus, a straight flush with 2◇, 3◇, 4◇, 5◇, 6◇
loses to a straight flush with 3♠, 4♠, 5♠, 6♠, 7♠.

FOUR OF A KIND: Four aces beats four kings and so on.

FULL HOUSE: A hand containing three cards of one rank or denomination and two cards of another denomination, such as
10, 10, 10, 8, 8. Where two full houses compete, the higher
three of a kind is the winner, so that K, K, K, 2, 2 beats Q, Q,
Q, J, J, and 4, 4, 4, 5, 5 beats 3, 3, 3, K, K.

FLUSH: Any five cards of the same suit (clubs, diamonds, etc.)
which are not a straight flush. Where two flushes compete,
the rank of the highest card wins, without regard to the
other four cards in the flush. Thus A♡, 9♡, 4♡, 3♡, 2♡ beats
K♠, Q♠, J♠, 9♠, 8♠.

STRAIGHT: Five cards in sequence. An ace may be in either a
high straight or a low straight (A, 2, 3, 4, 5). The rank of the
highest card in the straight determines the winner when two
straights compete. A 10-high straight beats an 8-high straight.

THREE OF A KIND: The higher rank, of course, wins when two
hands with three of a kind compete. Thus three queens beats
three jacks.

Two PAIR: When two or more hands with two pair compete, the rank of the higher pair determines the winner. Therefore A, A, 2, 2, 3 beats Q, Q, 10, 10, 7.

ONE PAIR: The higher rank wins; a pair of queens beats a pair of jacks. When two players have the same pair, the rank of the highest of the remaining three cards determines the winner, so that 7, 7, A, 6, 5 beats 7, 7, K, Q, J.

No PAIRS: Highest card wins. A, Q, 4, 3, 2 beats both K, Q, J, 10, 8 and also A, J, 7, 6, 5.

Part 2—Low hands *

6 4 3 2 A (perfect)	8 4 3 2 A	8 7 4 3 2
6 5 3 2 A	8 5 3 2 A	8 7 5 2 A
6 5 4 2 A	8 5 4 2 A	8 7 5 3 A
6 5 4 3 A	8 5 4 3 A	8 7 5 3 2
7 4 3 2 A (perfect 7)	8 5 4 3 2	8 7 5 4 A
7 5 3 2 A	8 6 3 2 A	8 7 5 4 2
7 5 4 2 A	8 6 4 2 A	8 7 5 4 3
7 5 4 3 A	8 6 4 3 A	8 7 6 2 A
7 5 4 3 2	8 6 4 3 2	8 7 6 3 A
7 6 3 2 A	8 6 5 2 A	8 7 6 3 2
7 6 4 2 A	8 6 5 3 A	8 7 6 4 A
7 6 4 3 A	8 6 5 3 2	8 7 6 4 2
7 6 4 3 2	8 6 5 4 A	8 7 6 4 3
7 6 5 2 A	8 6 5 4 2	8 7 6 5 A
7 6 5 3 A	8 6 5 4 3	8 7 6 5 2
7 6 5 3 2	8 7 3 2 A	8 7 6 5 3
7 6 5 4 A	8 7 4 2 A	9 4 3 2 A
7 6 5 4 2	8 7 4 3 A	etc.

* Note that these hands may not be cards of the same suit. A flush is a flush in high-low poker; a seven-card-stud hand with J♠, 9♠, 6♣, 4♣, 3♣, 2♣, A♣ is a flush for high and a 9, 4 low. The same applies to a straight, as 2, 3, 4, 5, 6, Q, K is a straight for high and Q, 5 for low.

Appendix D

Glossary

ANNOUNCE—to declare or announce high or low at the conclusion of the betting in a high-low game.

ANTE—the money each player puts into the pot to play the hand. The dealer may ante for all players. This speeds up the game and avoids confusion.

BACK-TO-BACK—in five-card stud or a similar game, the down card and first up card are a pair (same as "wired").

BEATS ME—an expression indicating that a player concedes that he is beaten and folds.

BET—a player puts chips into the pot.

BLUFF—a player bets or raises to create the impression of a strong hand which he does not have.

BOBTAIL STRAIGHT—a four-card straight open at both ends. For example, 9, 10, J, Q and the draw of an 8 or K will make a straight. Ordinarily a better prospect than a draw to an inside straight.

BULLET (OR BULL)—an ace.

BUMP—to raise or increase the amount bet by the previous player.

BUST—a very poor hand.

BUSTED FLUSH—a four flush that failed to improve.

BUSTER—the card dealt does not improve the hand. A player with A, 3, 6 up is dealt a K. As the dealer turns the card he may refer to the K as a buster.

CALL—a player bets an amount equal to the bet of the player to his right; he calls or sees the bet. A player has three options once a bet has been made. He may call, fold, or raise.

CASE—in the expression "He drew the case deuce." The only deuce remaining in the deck. The other three deuces were exposed earlier in the hand.

CHASE—staying in a pot when it is necessary to improve the hand in order to win.

CHIP—a circular disk used to represent money. Chips are usually blue, red and white. It is ordinarily more convenient to use chips rather than money.

CINCH—a certain winner in a particular situation. A hand which cannot be beaten.

COURT CARD—a king, queen or jack. Synonymous with Picture card.

CUT—after shuffling and prior to dealing, a player who has not shuffled the cards divides the deck into two segments, and the segment from the bottom is placed at the top.

DEAD—in the expression "The 6s are dead." All 6s are exposed on the table, or some are on the table and the remaining 6s were turned by players who folded earlier in the hand.

DEAL—to distribute the cards to the players one at a time in a clockwise direction. Also means one game, or hand, or pot. "We'll deal one more hand" uses "deal" as a verb. "We'll play one more deal" uses "deal" as a noun.

DEALER'S CHOICE—a poker session in which the dealer may select the game to be played. His choice may sometimes be limited to a particular group of games.

DEALER'S GAME—a poker game in which the dealer has a slight advantage.

DECLARE—to declare or announce high or low at the conclusion of the betting.

DEEP SEVEN—a low such as 7, 5, 3, 2, A or 7, 5, 4, 2, A. A 7, 6 low is not a deep seven and a 7, 4, 3, 2, A is a perfect seven.

DEUCE—a two (2).

DOWN CARD—a card dealt face down in stud-poker games.

DRAW—the name of a poker game. As a verb, to draw, exchange, trade or substitute by discarding one or more cards and receiving new cards in place of the discards.

DROP OUT—to concede a hand by dropping out of it. The player is unwilling to call the bet.

FATTEN—from the expression "Fatten up the pot." A raise, bet or call which increases the size of the pot.

FLUSHING—a prospect of making a flush.

FOLD—to drop out of a hand by folding or turning the up cards. The player is unwilling to call the bet.

FOUR FLUSH—four in a suit (hearts, diamonds, clubs or spades).

FREE RIDE—all players check a round of betting. They receive the next card "free."

GOODIE—a card which probably improves a hand. The opposite of a buster.

GUTS TO OPEN—a variation of draw poker in which a player may open the betting on any holding. A more liberal game compared with jacks or better to open.

HAND—has two meanings. It may refer to the cards dealt to one player: "I held the best hand." Also it may mean a game: "I held the best low in the hand."

HIGH-LOW—a poker game in which the high poker hand and the lowest poker hand split the pot.

HOG IT—a player tries to hog the pot by announcing both high and low.

HOLE CARD—a card dealt face down in stud-poker games.

HOOK—a jack.

IMMORTAL—a hand which cannot be beaten in the given circumstances.

INSIDE STRAIGHT—an attempt to draw the final card to a straight in the "middle." Holding 6, 7, 8, 10 and attempting to get a 9. A poor play in most circumstances.

JACKPOTS—a game of draw poker in which a pair of jacks or better is required to start the betting.

JOKER—an extra (53rd) card used in some games. The meaning or value of the joker may vary. It may be wild or it may be treated as an ace and as a wild card only to make a straight or flush.

KICKER—a card in addition to a pair or three of a kind; in 6, 6, A the A is a kicker.

KITTY—a small amount is withdrawn from each pot and held in a kitty. The kitty is divided evenly at the conclusion of the evening. This is a method of reducing losses.

LIGHT—as in the expression, "I'm a dime light." A player out of chips plays on credit. He withdraws chips from the pot and holds them separately as a means of noting how much he owes the pot.

LIMIT—the largest amount a player may bet in a limit-stakes game.

LIMIT STAKES—the amount a player can bet or raise is limited by conventions of the game.

LOCK—a certain winner in a particular situation.

LOST ME—a player folds and says, "You lost me."

MATCH THE POT—in "baseball" a requirement to put into the pot the amount already in the pot on drawing a trey.

NO LIMIT—a player may bet any amount he wishes with no limitation of any kind (*see also* "table stakes").

OPEN AT BOTH ENDS—four cards in sequence which can be improved to a straight by drawing either of two cards—6, 7, 8, 9 can make a straight with a 5 or 10. A "bobtail straight."

OVER—as in the expression "Nines over"; a poker hand with two pair of which 9s are the higher pair (such as 9, 9, 7, 7, K).

PAT—as in the expression "Pat hand"; the player does not choose to draw or substitute. He plays the cards he holds at that point. In draw poker, an indication (actual or a bluff) that the hand cannot be improved. The minimum pat hand in draw is a straight.

PERFECT—a perfect low: 6, 4, 3, 2, A (it's lovely).

PICTURE CARD—a king, queen or jack. A "Court card."

POT—the money in the center of the table which has been bet as the hand progressed.

POT LIMIT—the amount a player may bet or raise is the sum of money or chips in the pot at the time he must bet. If there are 20 chips in the pot, the high player may bet up to 20 chips. If two others call, there will be 80 chips in the pot, which becomes the limit on the next bet. If the next bet is 80, the second player may call the 80 and raise 160, which was the amount in the pot at his turn. The third man may call for 240 chips and he may raise any amount up to 400, which was the amount in the pot at his turn.

POT RIGHT—the dealer inquires if all have called the bet before he proceeds to deal the next card. He asks whether the pot is as it should be.

PUSH—passing unwanted cards to the player to one's left.

RAISE—a player increases the amount bet when it is his turn.

RAT-HOLE—a player pockets some of his money or chips. In table stakes this limits the amount he is willing to risk in a single pot.

ROUND—in the expression "Let's play one more round." A series of hands in which each player deals once.

RUN ONE—an attempt to win a pot by bluffing.

SANDBAG—this expression is derived from the notion of dropping a heavy bag of sand on an unwary opponent after having lulled him into a false sense of security by an earlier indication of weakness. You check on your first opportunity to bet and when an opponent bets you raise; or you merely call a bet but when this is raised by an opponent to your left you raise when it comes back to you.

SELLING—in the expression "I'm selling." The dealer indicates he is ready to deal a substitution round in three-card substitution or a similar game where a substitution may be made for a fee.

SEQUENTIAL DECLARATION—a method of declaring high or low in which the last raiser or the bettor announces first and others declare high or low in a clockwise direction.

SHUFFLE—to mix the cards by riffling or by hand-over-hand mixing.

SHY—same as "light." A player out of chips plays on credit for the balance of a hand. He designates the amount he is shy by withdrawing chips from the pot. If he loses the hand, he "squares up" by purchasing chips from a player or the banker.

SIMULTANEOUS DECLARATION—a method of declaring high or low. Players take two chips and move both hands under the table. They return one clenched fist to the center of the table. When the dealer announces "open," all players unclench their fist. The absence of a chip is a low call; one chip is a high call; both chips is a two-way call.

SPIT—a card turned face up in the center which may be used by all players.

STAND PAT—the player rejects the opportunity to draw or exchange cards. He chooses to play the cards he holds.

STAY—to stay in a hand by calling or paying the amount already bet.

STRAIGHTING—a prospect of making a straight.

STUD—a family of poker games in which some of the cards are dealt up.

SUBSTITUTION—an exchange of cards. The player discards a card and receives one from the deck to replace it.

SWEETEN—any action which increases the size of the pot.

TABLE STAKES—a poker game in which a player may bet any amount up to the total of the chips or money he has on the table in front of him. He may not increase or reduce the amount he has on the table once a hand has started.

TAP—an expression in table stakes which means, "I bet all the chips I have on the table." The maximum amount a player may bet.

TAP YOU—when the person who must bet has more chips than his opponent, "tap you" means that he bets the number of chips his opponent has on the table.

TICKETS—cards. As in the expression "I held some good tickets."

TRADE—to trade a card or substitute by discarding and receiving a replacement.

TREY—a three (3).

Two-way call—a player declares both high and low. He must win both or he loses both.

Two-way hand—a holding which has a possibility of winning both the high and the low in a pot.

Undercut—in low-hole-card-wild games, the final card is lower than the original hole cards and changes the wild card unfavorably.

Up—as in the expression "tens up." A poker hand with two pair of which 10s are the higher pair. (Same as "over"—"tens over.")

Whipsaw—a powerful high and a strong low raise the maximum number of times permitted, and a third player is trapped and calls all the raises.

Wild card—a card which can be used for any suit and any denomination.

Wired—in five-card stud or a similar game, a down card and first up card are a pair. The same as back-to-back.

About the Author

Irv Roddy is the pseudonym of a U.S. Government statistician and economist. He was born in Chicago, where he attended public schools and obtained a degree in economics from the University of Chicago. Mr. Roddy's hobbies, in addition to poker, are bridge, pinochle and American history. Employed in Washington for the past twenty years, he lives in nearby Maryland with his wife and three children. This is Irv Roddy's first book.